MAKING THE MOST OF YOUR MILESTONE BIRTHDAY

SECOND
EDITION

Things to Do When You Turn 40

Edited by Ronnie Sellers

SELLERS
PUBLISHING

Sellers Publishing, Inc.

161 John Roberts Road, South Portland, Maine 04106

Visit our Web site: www.sellerspublishing.com

E-mail: rsp@rsvp.com

Ronnie Sellers: President and Publisher

Mary Baldwin: Managing Editor

Charlotte Cromwell: Production Editor

ISBN 13: 978-1-4162-4667-1

Library of Congress Control Number: 2018951944

Printed and bound in the United States of America.

Credits: *What to know about turning 40* (p. 208) © 2013 Samantha Ettus. This essay originally appeared in ForbesWoman. *How to Survive Your 40s* (p. 200) © 2018 Pamela Druckerman. Excerpt from *There Are No Grown-Ups: A Midlife Coming-Of-Age Story* by Pamela Druckerman, copyright © 2018 by Pamela Druckerman. Used by permission of Penguin Press, an imprint of Penguin Publishing Group, a division of Penguin Random House LLC. All rights reserved.
Credits continued on page 240.

Contents

SECTION ONE
Speak Your Truth

Italian poet Cesare Pavese wrote, "From the moment you turn 40, you are responsible for your own face." Novelist Tawni O'Dell expands on this truth through personal reflection and the discovery that only you can decide who you will be.

Renowned CEO and best-selling author of *Fat, Forty & Fired*, Nigel Marsh believes turning 40 provides a natural milestone that people can use as a prompt to take a step back from their hurried everyday schedules and assess their lives.

After she spent three years crisscrossing the country to learn about fanatics, this columnist and writer urges you to find your passion, no matter how big or small, and pursue it relentlessly.

Novelist and short story writer Tim Hall argues the finer points of turning a midlife crisis into a midlife opportunity.

This writer, performer, and ex-corporate executive details six maxims to live by now that you've turned the big 4-0.

Internationally recognized life coach and inspirational speaker Scott Chesney theorizes that the mind thinks, but that it's the heart that knows the truth.

This Broadway diva decided to make choices that reflected her real-life character, and it paid off in the world and on the stage.

Section Two
Gain New Goals

SECTION FIVE
The Substance of Style

SECTION SIX
Keep it in Balance

Introduction

You are turning 40 and I'll be up front with you. You won't get much sympathy from me, nor should you expect much sympathy from my fellow (100 million) baby boomers, all of who turned 40 long before you did.

Why should we feel sorry for you? Gravity hasn't started messing with you very much. Your skin hasn't wrinkled to any noticeable extent. You can still make it through the night without having to get up to relieve yourself. You don't spend countless hours wandering around in search of reading glasses, nor do you have any problem figuring out how to send text messages on your cell phone. Hell, the AARP hasn't even begun to try to hunt you down (although, whether you realize it or not, they've probably picked up on your scent). From our perspective, you've still got it pretty good.

Besides, yesterday I read that a well known actress announced "40 is the new 20." Her proclamation was not heavily covered by the media, which mystifies me because it certainly represents a major milestone in the effort to extend human longevity.

Apparently, as several of the authors who contributed essays for this book will corroborate, this happened in stages. First, 40 became the new 30. This was bothersome enough for those of us who had passed this milestone years before and didn't get to have our ages reduced by ten years. For us, forty wasn't the "new" anything. We weren't creative enough, or audacious enough, to claim that we'd managed to turn back time. In fact, quite the opposite was true. For the most part we considered 40 to be the beginning of "old." If we were uptight about turning

40 we took the easy way out. We lied about our age.

Now, to add insult to injury, 40 has been further reduced . . . by another ten years! If this trend continues, it won't be long before people turning 40 will be the age equivalent of middle schoolers!

If you ask me, all of this adds up to a pretty rosy picture for you soon-to-be 40-year-olds. You get the benefit of 40 years of life experiences while looking no different than you did in college! It's like a 50% rebate on your life!

As the publisher of *40 Things To Do When You Turn 40*, however, I must admit that when I learned that 40 had become the new 20, I became a bit nervous about how sales might be impacted. If turning 40 had really become such a non-issue, why would anyone bother to buy this book?

My fears were assuaged when I went back and reread the essays that our 40-something authors so generously provided, many of which describe in vivid (and often hilarious) detail the midlife crisis the writer experienced around the age of 40.

Apparently, despite the "new math" that reduces 40 by half and the advancements in cosmetic surgery that make it easier to fool the brain into thinking it's not getting any older, the psyche knows better . . . and the psyche ain't buying any of it! You might not be ready, willing, or able to admit it yet, but deep down inside, turning 40 still scares the hell out of you, and (whether you like it or not) it's almost inevitable that you, too, will have a midlife crisis!

While my ability to empathize with you is inhibited by my preoccupation with my own miserable age-related problems, I will acknowledge that you are facing issues that are relatively unique to your generation. If you are a woman, for instance, you may have been so focused on your career that you forgot (or opted not) to become a mother . . . or perhaps even someone's wife or domestic partner. Now your biological clock is ticking so loudly that you can't get any sleep. This is a phenomenon that is addressed by several of our writers.

If you are a man, you might have signed a ten-year lease on your soul in exchange for stock options in the next big Internet thing. Now, at age 40, you learn what Nigel Marsh admits in his essay he learned, "that you are working hard at a job you hate to buy things you don't need to impress people you don't like."

Of course everyone who is turning 40 must deal with the fact that the ice caps are melting. Previous generations may have had to worry about reducing waistlines at this age, but yours is the first to have to worry about reducing both waistlines and carbon footprints simultaneously.

To top it all off, there's the issue of your finances. How do you save for the future when it costs $2500 a month to rent a broom closet in Manhattan and you're still paying off your student loans? What happens if (when?) government sponsored medical services, entitlements, and pension funds go bust? If this occurs, then "40 is the new 20" might seem more like a curse than a blessing

How do you deal with all of this? Well, that's where this book comes in. The celebrities, pundits, financial wizards, medical specialists, and theologians who wrote for it provide a wealth of information on the subject of turning 40. When taken in its entirety, the book is a comprehensive instruction manual for those who would like to make the process as meaningful, enjoyable, profitable, and healthy as possible.

I am not giving anything away by saying the message the book leaves you with is a very positive one: If you approach the experience of turning 40 as an opportunity to take stock of your life, ask difficult questions, and (if you don't like the answers) start making changes, then the second half of your life will almost certainly be happier and more fulfilling than the first. And who knows, perhaps by the time you turn 50 it will be the new 25!

Ronnie Sellers

Section One

SPEAK YOUR TRUTH

Take me at face value

Italian poet Cesare Pavese wrote, "From the moment you turn 40, you are responsible for your own face." Novelist Tawni O'Dell expands on this truth through personal reflection and the discovery that only you can decide who you will be.

by Tawni O'Dell

Tawni O'Dell is the *New York Times* bestselling author of six novels including *Sister Mine, Coal Run,* and *Back Roads,* which was an Oprah's Book Club pick and a Book-of-the-Month Club Main Selection. *Back Roads* is currently in development to be made into a film. Tawni was born and raised in the coal-mining region of western Pennsylvania, where she has returned and now lives with her two children.

I don't belong to a book club myself. But as a fairly well known best-selling author who lives in a small town in Pennsylvania — as someone who mows her own yard and has two children in the public school system who play sports and constantly need rides — I'm not exactly an inaccessible recluse. I've been accosted in the grocery store, at my son's soccer games, leaving a movie theater, and once even had a woman slow down her SUV as she drove past my front yard where I was raking leaves and shout out an invitation to me. I am often approached by total strangers who ask me to attend book club meetings where they're scheduled to discuss one of my novels.

The other night I was sitting at one of these meetings in a spotless living room, sipping a glass of pink wine, listening to the chatter going on around me. This particular book club was made up of women in their 20s and 30s. At 43, I was by far the oldest one there.

The conversations weren't really what I'd call conversations. There was no exchange of ideas. They were more along the lines of verbal competitions where the point was to vocally bludgeon each other with ever bigger and ever wilder claims of what they owned, how well they maintained their faces, and how exhausted they were. As I listened it suddenly struck me that the reason I wasn't participating wasn't because I didn't own things or because I didn't have a face or because I wasn't inordinately perky that evening. It was because I didn't care to discuss any of the things they were discussing. Not so long ago I would have tried to make myself care, or I would have worried that I didn't care, or I would have pretended that I cared. Now I calmly revel in the fact that I don't care that I don't care.

To me this has been one of the best discoveries about entering my 40s: I've reached a place where I no longer feel the need to try and impress everyone I meet by listing everything I have and everything I do. If someone is going to be impressed by me I want it to be because of who I am.

I suppose it's no surprise that in a society that thrives on competition and gives everything a rating, we as members of this society come to think that our value lies solely in a laundry list of our accomplishments and assets. It's only with age and experience that we begin to question the lack of sense and humanity behind this assumption.

I decided not to be so judgmental of these women and made a few quick mental lists of my own priorities at their ages.

Things I cared about in my 20s: straightening my hair, the color of my car, finding a man, always being right, dressing sexy, wondering what I'm going to be when I grow up, Don Johnson.

Things I cared about in my 30s: being a good mom, being a good wife, being a good writer, being a good daughter, being a good lover, being a good friend, being a good citizen.

Things I care about in my 40s: sleep, avoiding rudeness, finding some time away from my man, jazz, feeling sexy, wondering when I get to stop being what I finally ended up being when I grew up, calcium.

I was self-absorbed in my 20s; my 30s were full of self-sacrifice. But underlying both was the need to impress people, whether it be with how I looked or how I lived or how much I was doing for others.

I took my analysis one step further and decided that the 20s are the Decade of the Ego: Look at me. The 30s are the Decade of the Martyr: Look at What I'm Doing. The 40s are the Decade of Acceptance: You May Look at Me . . . But Also Talk to Me.

One of my favorite lines about turning 40 comes from the Italian poet, Cesare Pavese, who wrote, "From the moment you turn 40, you are responsible for your face."

He wrote this more than 60 years ago so I'm pretty sure he wasn't talking about Botox, or chemical peels, or nose jobs.

For me what he's saying is 40 is the age when you finally take matters into your own hands, and you decide what you will be and who you will be. Other people's opinions and approval aren't tantamount anymore. What matters is your opinion. You're in charge of what kind of face you're going to show the world because frankly, the world is beginning to not care about you.

You've reached your 40s. You're a real grown-up now.

Your mistakes aren't as readily forgiven. Excuses aren't accepted. Your future is not as wide open as it used to be. No one is going to tell you, "You've got your whole life ahead of you," ever again.

As I looked around the room at all the young fresh faces eager to dominate yet also eager to be loved, I thought of the beginning of a sculpture when the clay is still wet and anyone who walks by can take it into his hands and mold it into something he wants it to be.

I'm at a point now where that clay is beginning to dry. I offer resistance to those hands. I'm taking on my permanent shape. There's still a little work to be done. There are still some changes to be made just as there still will be changes in my life, but my basic form will remain the same. Soon I will be completely set, and I take comfort in knowing that once I am, I will be able to weather the worst storms and the brightest days and keep my integrity intact like any work of art.

I settled back into my chair knowing soon we would start discussing a novel, and those conversations always shed light on a person's true self. *What kind of person are you?* That's the query we'll be asking each other with each question from the Reader's Guide. This *is* something we should care about. Possibly it's the only thing. ⇐

Pause for reflection

Renowned CEO and best-selling author of *Fat, Forty &
Fired*, Nigel Marsh believes turning 40 provides a natural
milestone that people can use as a prompt to take
a step back from their hurried everyday schedules
and assess their lives.

by Nigel Marsh

Nigel Marsh is the bestselling author of *Fat, Forty, and Fired* —
his frank, funny and inspiring memoir that details how he used his
40th birthday as a catalyst to radically change and improve his life.
He is also the author of three additional books *Observations of a Very
Short Man, Overworked and Underlaid* and *Fit, Fifty and Fired-Up.*
Nigel is a sought-after public speaker and a renowned business
leader. Currently CEO of strategic consultancy WEST82nd, Nigel
is working on the TV adaptation of *Fat, Forty, and Fired.* He lives
with his wife and four children in Sydney, Australia. To learn more
visit his website at www.nigelmarsh.com.

The fifth-century mystic St Benedict wasn't talking
specifically to 40 year olds when he memorably
advised his followers to "pause for a moment you wretched
weaklings and take stock of your miserable existence,"
but it is advice that I feel is particularly relevant to those

approaching the milestone of completing their fourth decade. In modern life it is so easy to get caught up just "doing" — particularly as a young adult trying to make his or her way in the world — bending all your energies and talents to surviving and providing for your loved ones it is possible to unwittingly lose sight of the type of life that you actually want to live.

A pause for reflection at 40 is a wonderful idea. This reflection hasn't got to involve a break from the workforce as it did for me — it can take place over one evening. The only requirement is total honesty with yourself. Don't be scared when you do this. No one else need ever learn of your true feelings and, indeed, you need never act on them. All you have to do, just this once, is to ask yourself fearlessly "do I like the life I am leading and the type of person I have become?" Don't worry about acting on your conclusions. For now all you are doing is thinking honestly about the questions. Try and listen with the "ear of your heart" and shut out all of societies' overt and covert pressures and expectations.

If you discover, as I did, that you are working hard at a job you hate to buy things you don't need to impress people you don't like, then I humbly suggest some more reflection may be in order. If you discover everything is exactly how you want it to be then you've simply spent a pleasant evening confirming your life's path.

For the rest of us, however, it can be a rude awakening. Do you know the names of any of your children's friends? Can you remember the last time you had sex sober? Do you contribute to the community you live in or is your sole focus on your own personal well being and happiness?

In my case I realized that I was the classic corporate warrior — eating too much, drinking too much, working too hard, and neglecting my family. I was postponing my life. I also realized that the cliché is true — this isn't a dress rehearsal. If you don't design the life you want, someone else will design it for you.

The wonderful thing about turning 40 is that it doesn't let you off the hook. When you are younger you can kid yourself that you are only living an unsatisfactory life "for the time being." Once you've "got a few things sorted" then you'll change. At 40 there is no more room for denial — the life you are living IS you. At the age of 40 it is slightly tragic to pretend to yourself and to others that you are going to change things in the future. There's no point attempting to get to know your wife after she's divorced you or trying to connect with your kids after they have left home. The model of "I'll have a life when I retire" is a damaging lie. You won't have any friends or interests — it will be too late. NOW is the time. You are 40 not 20. It really is now or never.

For me this reflection involved turning the telescope around and putting the things I valued at the center of my life not at the edges. There's a wonderful Buddhist phrase "before enlightenment — chop wood, carry water. After enlightenment? — chop wood, carry water." Like the rest of us I still had to live in the real world and make a living, but I did it with a different focus and a different set of priorities. I'm not advising anyone to kick it all in and go to live in a cave (unless you want to). I am advising that you start to take yourself, your dreams, and your inner desires seriously. After all no else is going to.

If I want to spend proper time with my wife, then working eleven hours a day and doing a three-hour daily commute isn't going to work. After reaching 40 in this scenario rather than giving up on my desire to have a meaningful regular relationship with my wife, I'll change my job.

If I want to be a loving, involved, and present father to my four young kids, waking up every Saturday morning with a crashing hangover isn't going to cut it. Again in this scenario after reaching 40 rather than giving up on the father role, I'll give up drinking.

Obviously everyone is different and I'm not pretending to be an expert here or have the answers. What I am saying is this: Putting one evening aside to spend on your own and think about your life on or around your 40th birthday is an investment that is well worth the effort.

It could save your life. It saved mine.

3

Embrace your inner passion

After she spent three years crisscrossing the country to learn about fanatics, this columnist and writer urges you to find your passion, no matter how big or small, and pursue it relentlessly.

by Shari Caudron

Shari Caudron is an award-winning columnist and professional writer whose articles and essays have appeared in *Reader's Digest, Christian Science Monitor, USA Today, Sunset Magazine,* and many other publications. She is the author of two books, the most recent of which is titled *Who Are You People? A Personal Journey into the Heart of Fanatical Passion in America.* She currently is a memoir and nonfiction book coach. To learn more visit her Web site at www.sharicaudron.com.

I was never one of those people who had a fanatical passion. I jumped from hobby to hobby, whether it was running or photography or belly dancing or snowshoeing. I even took fencing classes. Early on, I was content to hopscotch from one hobby to another. But then, right about the time I turned 40, I found myself starting to become jealous of people who weren't like me; of people who were passionately, fanatically *into* things. Things like fly fishing or Barbie collecting or going to Airstream conventions. I was jealous that these people *had* passions (which I did not) and could express them with any hint of apology or self-consciousness. How was this possible? What did these fanatics have that I didn't? I set out to find the answer.

I spent three years crisscrossing the country to learn about fanatics. I spent time with everyone from Barbie collectors and adult Lego users to storm chasers and Josh Groban fans. Along the way, I gained some insight into the nature of fanatical passion.

The number one thing that passion provides — and probably the most satisfying — is a sense of community and support. Never underestimate how important it is to find your tribe — that group of people who get you on that all-important level. By pursuing your passion, and seeking out others who share it, chances are good that you'll find your own supportive niche.

Connecting with like-minded fanatics also allows people to address two conflicting, but very important desires in life: to both fit in *and* be unique. By expressing your inner Barbie collector, for instance, you're allowing your uniqueness to shine through. But by gathering with other doll collectors, you can still be part of the crowd.

Our passions and fanatical pursuits also reflect deeply

held values. In other words, passions tell us what matters to us in life. On the surface, being an active fan of the Andy Griffith Television show may seem trivial. But ask an Andy Griffith fan *why* she's a fan, and she'll tell you that the show reminds her of the right, moral, kind way to live.

Passions often provide people with a revived sense of pride and achievement. Even if you already have an otherwise successful and fulfilling career, and certainly if you don't, pursuing your passion can offer accomplishments and self-respect in new and important ways. You might become the best ice fisherman in your town, or the person with the biggest collection of action heroes, or someone who has the most lush flower garden. It doesn't really matter what the pursuit is, only that is offers a sense of pride.

Why is age 40 a good time to indulge your passions? Because by 40, for the most part, we're settled in our careers and we're no longer putting the same energy toward getting a mate, or starting a family, or finding a house. By 40, many of those young adult activities have been taken care of. Because we're not working on building the foundation for our lives, our energy and attentions are freed up and we begin to realize that maybe we haven't been playing as much as we should, and that perhaps we've slipped into some kind of pattern or established routine. By 40, we have the time and luxury of asking ourselves — what really makes me happy?

Even if you think your interest or hobby isn't exactly a full-fledged passion, now might be a good time to explore it, seek it out, and find others who share your interest. Even if you have just a kernel of some interest, follow it to see where it leads you.

I spent three years researching fanatics around the country and trying to understand *other* people's passions. What I discovered is that while I don't have a passion as fanatical (at least on the face of it) as those of the people I met, I do have my own distinct passion. I am curious. I am passionate about learning new subjects and different ideas from varied people. I have embraced this fact and now indulge that curiosity whenever the mood strikes — by going to museums, plays, a new town, or countries I'd never considered. I also continue to write about people who strike my fancy.

While I still admire so-called fanatics, I've found that I'm no longer jealous of them. I found my passion. What is yours?

As told to Megan Hiller.

4

Midlife: don't call it a crisis

Novelist and short story writer Tim Hall argues the finer
points of turning a midlife crisis into a midlife opportunity.

by Tim Hall

Writer, multimedia artist, novelist, and journalist Tim Hall is also
the producer of the cable TV show, "Story Time" broadcast to more
than 80,000 homes in the Chicago area. He is the author of two
novels *Half Empty* and *Full Of It* and a collection of short stories
titled *Triumph of the Won't*.

Shortly after my 40th birthday I met my friend
Brian for lunch. He noticed right away that I wasn't
my usual sunny, irrepressible self. "What's wrong?" he
asked.

"Brian, I'm having a midlife crisis," I said.

"How do you know?"

"Look at me. I'm wearing Birkenstock sandals with a
Ramones T-shirt."

"Good point."

My friend just happens to be a brilliant college professor, so he quickly took the intellectual approach.

"Tim," he said to me, "did you know that in the Chinese language, the symbol for 'crisis' is the same as the one for 'opportunity'?"

"Yes," I replied, "and did you know it is also the same as the symbol for 'Harley-Davidson'?"

Okay, so according to Brian I'm not having a midlife crisis. I'm having a midlife opportunity. I don't mean to pick on my friend. The problem is that he's too young to understand what I'm going through; after all, he's only a baby of 38. Once you hit that giant cinderblock wall of 40 things begin to look a whole lot different. They look blurrier, for starters.

As I thought about what he said, however, I began to realize that he was right. The fact is, I'm having a great midlife opportunity so far, with very little crisis. I always thought a guy my age was supposed to buy a red sports car and run off with the secretary. In fact, I'm pretty sure the Japanese word for midlife crisis is "Miata." Men don't have secretaries anymore; when a man hits 40 nowadays he's expected to start an angry political blog about Important Things, like war and terrorism and the decline of a once-great nation that no longer provides its middle-aged men with young secretaries. All this ranting and raving, of course, must be done on a wireless laptop from an undisclosed cul-de-sac, while washing down bags of Chee-zee Snax with Ultra Lite beer. Not me. I'm a rebel until the end, in my Ramones T-shirts and orthopedic sandals. I'm taking the only viable route open to a real man my age — which is to say, I 'll do whatever reasonable thing my wife thinks is best.

As a result, we recently made a graceful transition from my hometown of New York City to a quiet river town in the Midwest. I've been giving this a lot of thought, and I realize now that New York City is a very bad place to have a midlife crisis. Midlife crises are all about making one last stab at some semblance of autonomy and purpose in life, at least before we start opening those envelopes from the AARP that started showing up in the mail, ominously, around our 35th birthdays. We want to feel that there's some period of time, between the cluelessness of youth and the infirmity of old age, that we have real freedom and control over our own destinies. Academics like my friend Brian call this sense of freedom and control "agency" — which is just a fancy way of saying, "whatever reasonable thing our wives think is best." The key word to keep in mind here, I think, is not agency but expansion: As the lines on our faces grow along with our waistlines, so must our lives and minds and sense of possibilities. It's very hard to expand in New York, where a parking space rents for more than a good-sized house in much of the rest of the country, and a half million dollars buys you something the size of an airplane bathroom.

Now, some of you might be thinking that pulling up stakes from my hometown and moving four states away, to a small town in the Midwest, might constitute a different kind of midlife crisis, and you might be right about that, except for one important factor. You see, in the old days, the reason men like me ran off with their secretaries was because after college they rushed right out and got respectable jobs, married, and moved to the suburbs and started having kids — so that, by the time they were 35, they were starting to look like the *Man in the Gray Flannel Suit,* only without Gregory Peck's cheekbones. They only began questioning the meaning of their lives once it was already too late.

I was smarter about it: by waiting, and timing my move to the suburbs to coincide with my midlife crisis — which hits every one of us sooner or later, whether we want it to or not — I was able to blunt the harshest effects. Now, instead of gnashing my teeth and wondering what the meaning of life is, I gnash my teeth and wonder where the hell the exit to the stupid mall parking lot is. Forget existential crisis — I have an exit-stential crisis almost every day. I seem perfectly able to find my way into the malls, but never can find my way out. I'm beginning to think that when I'm in Trader Joe's or Target there are actually teams of parking lot elves who come and move the concrete dividers around just to confuse me. It's enough to make me want to buy a riding mower and wireless laptop, and start an angry political blog about how the modern shopping mall parking lot is proof positive that this country is finally, irrevocably, going down the tubes.

So, if you're looking for me, I'll be the paunchy guy at the end of the cul-de-sac, surrounded by bags of Cheezee snax and empty cans of Ultra Lite Beer, furiously typing away with fluorescent orange thumbs. But then I realize, if that's the worst of it, then I'm really doing all right. In fact, the more I think about it, the more convinced I become that I'm going to have a wonderful midlife crisis. Or, if you listen to my friend Brian, midlife opportunity. Or, if you believe the Chinese, midlife motorcycle.

5

Don't be a jerk

This writer, performer, and ex-corporate executive details
six maxims to live by now that you've turned the big 4-0.

by Steve Belanger

After a 16-year, soul-crushing career as a corporate executive,
Steve Belanger found salvation, if not steady income, in a life of
writing and performing. He has worked with Oscar-winners. He
has written countless scripts. His work has appeared in several
major magazines. He has performed comedy on the country's most
celebrated stages. And he's willing to share his secrets with you.

Ahhh, the f-word. Not the one that will get you in
trouble. Well, actually this one might get you in
trouble depending on how you wield it. I'm speaking of
course about the word f-f-f-orty. Forty years old is not as
hard to get to as you would think. After the slow-motion
uphill struggle that is your teens, 40 hunts you down
like that shark in *Jaws*. Twenties are a blur as you make
the hairpin turn past 30, buzzing right over the speed-
bump that is 35 until you find yourself turning 39. "One
more year," you say to yourself, "I've got one more year

of being in my 30s and I am going to make the most of it!" Then you wake up a few hours later and you're wearing a silly birthday hat while people are handing you cards about being over the hill and you're staring at a birthday cake with two big wax candles on it. One, of course, is a four and the other is a zero. So there it is, your 40. F----! [expletive deleted]

Turning 40 wasn't terribly difficult to me, because I couldn't quite grasp it. I was still a bumbling teenager at heart. Maybe not the naïve, young clueless oaf of my early teens, but something in the 17- to 18-year-old range where I was starting to understand how the world worked, but just couldn't figure out how to solidify my place in it. That was me then. And that's still me now.

I'll tell you how I got here, more as a cautionary tale than a handbook. As they say in the car commercials in really small print "closed roads do not attempt." Think of my life as closed roads down which you should not follow. Unless you want to. I mean, I'm having a hell of a good time. Who's to say it won't work for you. [Lawyer's note: It won't work for you. Get a real job. These roads are closed.]

These are the maxims I try to live my life by.

#1 – Don't be a jerk.

This one seems easy, but it's not. How many jerks do

you know? See what I mean? Midway through my 30s I realized that I was turning into a world-class jerk. I was taking out career frustrations on the one person who deserved it least, my loving wife. I got stuck in a career path I hadn't chosen and spent well over a decade convincing myself that the money I was making would quiet the tempest rising in my heart. "Wrong! Good try, thanks for playing." It is of course true that having money is easier than not having money, and as someone who grew up on food stamps and other government assistance I know a little bit about not having money. But now that I had enough to be financially stable for a while, I realized that the almighty buck is not the answer, which leads us to maxim #2.

#2 – There's never enough money.
There just isn't. There's never enough money to make things right. There's never enough money to create happiness. If money is all you think about, you'll never have enough. Whereas, if happiness is all you think about, you will always have more than you need. That sounds like New Age crap to me too, but it's true. I had an opportunity to take a huge risk when I was in my late 30s. Give up financial stability and a successful 16-year corporate career to pursue the dream of being an actor. Was it an easy decision? Not at all! I spent weeks of sleepless nights trying to decide if this was the right move. And you know how long it took to figure out if I'd

done the right thing? About 2 hours. That first Monday morning that I wasn't trudging into the office to kiss the asses of those lucky enough to have jobs above me and I knew that I was on the right path. My dream has yet to lead to wild success, and I'm realistic enough to know it probably never will, but every step of the journey has been incredibly rewarding and has enriched my life tremendously. It's kind of like those bumper stickers that say " The worst day of fishing is better than the best day of work!" Except not so corny.

#3 – Breathe.

Take the time to just breathe. Look around and actually acknowledge everything you have to be thankful for. I still have a tendency to get depressed if I'm up for a role and then don't get it. But then I realize how amazing it is that I can actually audition and do this stuff to begin with. And while mine is an extreme example, I'm sure there are similar things that you should be thankful for too that you overlook constantly. Go ahead, look around at all the things you take for granted on a daily basis. Take your time. I'll still be here when you get back.

#4 - Appreciate everything, regret nothing.

Appreciating everything should really be a subset under Maxim #3 "Breathe," But I like the way it sounded with the second half. "Appreciate everything, regret nothing," almost sounds like a Nike ad, right? [*Note to Nike marketing team: you may use this in your next campaign, as long as the commercials star a spry 40-something actor who occasionally writes essays about life lessons.] I have done plenty of stupid things in my life and had more than a fair share of crap done to me, but if I could suddenly go back in time and change anything, I wouldn't. Because everything that has happened has made me the person I am today, and unlike the first three decades or so of my life, I actually like me right now. So it's not like I completely disregard my past, but I certainly don't waste any effort with regret or what-ifs or anything else that is self-defeating in the here and now.

#5 – Keep it fresh

My wife and I have fun together. We always have and we always will. We make each other laugh and that, my friends, is truly the spice of life. We see so many couples who fall into the trap of taking each other for granted and it mystifies us. We have been married for almost 10 years now [lawyer's note: don't forget to buy her a nice anniversary present — see maxim #1], and we still enjoy each other's company as much as when we first started dating. Do not get into ruts. Do not let relationships get stale. Everything you do in life, "Keep it fresh."

#6 – Eat your veggies.

You're 40 now, you need your anti-oxidants.

So that's how I live my life. For the most part. I'm not always perfect, but I do my best. And I'm almost always happy. Plus, I play a lot of golf.

Now put this book down and go do something! There will be plenty of time to read when you're 70.

6

Ask your heart, not your head, where to go from here

Internationally recognized life coach and inspirational speaker Scott Chesney theorizes that the mind thinks, but that it's the heart that knows the truth.

by Scott Chesney

Scott Chesney, living with paralysis since the age of 15, is an internationally recognized life coach and keynote speaker who has addressed groups ranging from the United Nations to Fortune 500 corporations. Scott, who can be found on the Internet at www.scottchesney.com, has served on the Board of Trustees of Children's Specialized Hospital, the Advisory Board of the New Jersey Disability, Health, and Wellness program, and the Northern NJ Spinal Cord Injury System. In his spare time, he cherishes the moments spent with his wife and two children.

A friend of mine who's about to turn 40 just sent me an e-vite with the subject heading: "40 is the new 30!" Is this person in denial, trying to ease his way through a tough life transition? Maybe. But here's another possibility: The idea that anything is possible — that being 40 really *is* like being 30.

Tough to swallow? I thought so. But why? Because you're listening to your mind and your mind fears change.

Maybe you see your brain playing out a scenario that says, now that you're 40, you've scaled Mount Everest. It's time to come down from the mountain! Your time is up; you can find a boat at sea level and sail off into the sunset.

Not ready to do that? Good! Every time you hear an inner voice telling you that 40 is the start of a sunset voyage, you can just smile and know that it is just your mind talking.

"Well," you might respond, "my mind is what guides me. I can't ignore what my brain tells me!"

Maybe so, but how would you like to begin living in a place of unlimited potential, exponential growth, and boundless energy . . . starting at the age of 40? Sound like a plan? Well, it is a plan that the mind can't comprehend — so it will do everything in its power to reject the energy that drives it. What you must know is that on a much deeper level, located in the center of your chest — yes, your heart! — the plan is in your very best interest.

You see, the mind *thinks* but it's the heart that *knows*. The negative ideas you may have about what it means to turn 40 are preconceptions your mind creates. You need to put them in perspective by listening to your heart, as well as your mind. Why? Because the heart is the wellspring of all the accomplishment, happiness, and growth people achieve both before and *after* they reach their 40th birthday.

Your heart tells you that *anything is possible;* that age really is an accident of birth! How about right here, right now declaring to the world that today is a new beginning — that I am free to be me — and that I still have so much life left inside me! How liberating would that feel? All you have to do is say so. You have the power to choose.

A dear friend of mine once told me that we either evolve or dissolve. *Hmmm.* To me, dissolving sounds like a matter of the mind, while evolving sounds like a matter of the heart. I know that I am not ready to dissolve, so I fuel my evolution with gratitude. How do you do that? For one moment, imagine taking full responsibility for creating absolutely everything in your life that has brought you to the age of 40. Is this too difficult a task for you — or is it too daunting a task for your mind? Because I will tell you that there is no task that is too hard for your heart.

When we turn 40, many of us will go through a time of self-reflection. If we are operating from our minds, we'll probably sell ourselves short on what we have accomplished, achieved, or accumulated in our lives. It is the mind that discounts the need to celebrate the 40-year milestone. But if you listen to your heart, you'll see that each and every event that has transpired in your life has led you to this moment. So why would you want to change anything? The bumps and bruises along the way have all made you a stronger, more rounded person...if you choose to see it that way.

Forty is a time to celebrate the next step in the journey and acknowledge how far you've already come. The more you can be grateful in the present moment, the less likely will you choose to dwell on the past or become preoccupied with the future. Your time is now! What have you been putting off in your life that you know, in your heart, would bring you more peace and happiness? Now is the time to go for it!

Here's something to think about: You are walking along the beach and you stumble upon a magic lamp. You choose to rub the lamp and a genie appears, granting you three wishes on your 40th birthday. What will those three wishes be — and what is preventing you from pursuing these desires if you never stumble upon that magic lamp!

Enjoy the journey and welcome to 40...the new 30!

Divine your own right

This Broadway diva decided to make choices that reflected her real-life character, and it paid off in the world and on the stage.

by Tonya Pinkins

Tonya Pinkins is a multi-award winning American actor, director, educator and activist, and the author of *Get Over Yourself: How To Drop The Drama and Claim the Life You Deserve* (Hyperion Publishing). She's been nominated for three Tony awards for nine broadway shows and won the Tony for *Jelly's Last Jam*. At 40, she was named by Oprah as one of the "Ten Women in America Who Will Take Your Breath Away."

At 40, I was to play the greatest role of my career on Broadway in *Caroline or Change*. The opportunity had been a lifetime in the making. I believe it was accelerated by an intention I set a couple years earlier to only return to the stage in a show that would reflect my own character.

I had a reputation as a difficult Broadway Diva. The reality was that I had spent years controverting the truth in my heart by always trying to do what was right, or do what I was told. I had tried to play the "good girl" and failed. I said and did what I believed was expected of me. I forgot how to have an independent desire.

Caroline, a housemaid, was the title role. No good girl, no smiling maid, Caroline hated her job. She resented her employers and she let it be known to everyone.

I had never before played the lead. At 40, I was standing in a moment of great opportunity and peril. The show could rise or fall on my abilities. How could I do it right? And whose "right" was I to obey — the director's, my fellow actors', my mother's, my teachers', society's, my friends', God's?

I was involved in a lawsuit at the time and had decided that it was "right" to settle the case and give the plaintiff what he wanted. But when I came home after the settlement, I was enraged that I'd compromised and given up so much. So I berated myself. I felt that bitterness, like a gremlin, had taken hold of me, and I sought counsel to banish it from my spirit.

My spiritual adviser, a mystic Catholic nun, said "The gremlin is right." She told me that actions taken in denial of truth have no power and therefore cannot achieve their desired result. The truth was that I hadn't wanted to settle; I despised my accuser.

Although, at the time, I had believed I was doing the

right thing, my idea of right action was in opposition to my authentic, angry feelings. As if to confirm this revelation, my accuser threw out the settlement and proceeded with the lawsuit. Now I had to fight.

I had spent 40 years doing what I thought was right even when my soul cried out in protest. I realized that my anger, fear, and resistance bled through every supposed right action and robbed all my intended goodness of power. Now I had an opportunity to find my own right action — in harmony with my authentic feelings.

At 40, I didn't have to answer to anybody and I couldn't blame anybody either. Mama couldn't beat me. A teacher couldn't fail me. Friends and lovers could leave me. And employers could fire me — even when I thought I was doing right. So what did I have left: The responsibility to find the true Diva within me.

Instead of responding to the question "How are you?" with a temporal truth (I'm tired, I'm hungry, I'm ill….), I had often spoken the spiritual truth, "I am divine." But what did it mean to live the truth of my divinity? I believed that God was infinite and that God was within me. Yet, I had confined myself to preset behaviors and responses that denied the fullness of what I espoused as spiritual truth.

Now, I set a new intention to challenge every belief I

held which was not based on my own personal experience. Everything I said or did that was determined by someone else's idea of good and right was up for grabs. I set out to divine my own "right." I swapped "doing right" for being right "for me."

I allowed the pain and rage of my real life to flood through Caroline. It was big. It was scary. In the role, I found a place to express it all, and in that process, to heal myself. As my authentic feelings poured into Caroline on stage, a softer, gentler — yet more powerful — strength was expressed in my offstage life.

I tapped into a kind of knowing that poured forth from the diva within me. I divined that my instincts are right "for me." And to my surprise, my more authentic self was more in harmony with the world. The true diva shone forth with authentic opinions and with opposition, when it was called for, that was actually less adversarial than my "good girl."

My diva is more divine than any "good" person I can ever try to be. And I'd place my bets that yours is, too.

Renovate! (your inner spirit and your home)

Non-fiction author Michael Ruhlman believes you should acknowledge your core self at midlife. He explains how to rekindle your inner spirit by making a permanent change to your dwelling — inside or out.

by Michael Ruhlman

Michael Ruhlman is the author of *The Elements of Cooking*, *Boys Themselves*, *The Making of a Chef*, *The Soul of a Chef*, *The Reach of a Chef*, *Wooden Boats*, *Walk on Water*, *House: A Memoir* and *In Short Measures*. He has written numerous articles for *The New York Times*, the *Los Angeles Times*, *Gourmet*, *Saveur*, and *Food Arts* and was a judge for the Food Network's *The Next Iron Chef*.

I was 19 when I learned I should fear 40, an age that seemed to me about as far away as Pluto and just as relevant in my life. A psychology professor had noted to our class that 40 was a dividing age, an age at which adults reevaluated their lives. It was a time to accept the fact that many of our hopes and dreams simply weren't going to pan out, that the person who you'd become was not a person your 20-year-old self might even recognize. Forty was a time to reevaluate, abandon your former wished for self, cast off the goals that were clearly impossible, and set new goals. The professor said, "Some people even stage mock funerals." That was the detail that did it for me. The mock funeral — coffin, eulogies, and all. That was one serious 40th birthday party. Your old self is dead — who will you be now?

But 21 years later, 40 came and went for me. I was too busy with my children (a four-year-old and an eight-year-old), a 13-year-old marriage, and a 100-year-old house to care much about the actual day. The wife and I went out to dinner and got in a colossal, near-marriage-ending fight on the drive home. That was how I marked 40, and I don't recommend it.

So while I had no funeral of my own and didn't even pause for reflection on the occasion, I'd sensed back in college and sensed still that this mock funeral was right somehow. It was true. The age 40, a convenient halfway marker, deserved more consideration than any of the other decade benchmarks.

My recommendation, at age 40, is to build a fire pit. By 40 we have wrapped ourselves in numerous husks — I listed a few of mine above, the things that kept me from even acknowledging my 40-year-old self or caring about the day — the husk of fatherhood, husband, homeowner. My work, my persona as a writer, may be the biggest husk of all. We need to stop to remember and acknowledge our core selves, the boy, the girl who remains alive within our adult shell.

Fire can take us here. Build a pit and sit around a crackling fire deep into the night and watch the sparks fly into the black as your ancient forebearers did. Coat yourself in the smell of burning wood. Fall asleep outside or at least go to bed with the smoke and the ash of the fire on you. Acknowledge the atavistic core that remains a living thing within those many husks we've bundled ourselves in.

Of course it doesn't have to be fire — any substantial change to your dwelling (your house or the land around) — is an appropriate marker and celebration of the self, the living core at the center of the unchanging husks. In Jungian theory, houses in dreams are one of the few symbols of the complete psyche, the whole complex, layered, monster. To get into the interior of your house, whether into the ground to build a fire pit, or inside its walls, will be a meaningful physical change worth the effort. The act carries with it a spiritual recognition of self as well.

To mark 40, make a substantial permanent change to your dwelling. It should not be something you can do in an afternoon, but something that takes three or four weekends. It should be a task that is unfamiliar, one that forces you to research and study and plan. It should be complex enough that it requires good *mise en place*, a cook's term for organization, having all the ingredients and tools you'll need for the task at hand. Tear up the old linoleum or shag carpet and refinish the floorboards underneath. The act of tearing off a covering of something and renewing an original surface is exactly the spirit you want to give to the endeavor that marks the big 4 - 0.

Tear the paper from a useful wall in your kitchen and tile it. A dramatic alteration of one of the most important communal rooms of the house, the room where food is prepared, is also in the right spirit. Rip out an old ugly hearth and put in a new brick or stone one. I did this several months before I turned 40. We'd bought an old house and were slowly restoring it. The hearth bricks were buckling and coming lose and it was time to tackle the job. I ripped up the stone. I felt like I was working in the house's mouth, pulling out living but rotting pieces. In the moldering concrete beneath these bricks I found bones. Not chicken bones. Big enough to give you the eebie jeebies when you find them. I asked an orthopedic surgeon friend about them, and he turned them in his hands and said, "I don't know what they are, but I can tell you they aren't human."

A bone sleuth we knew guessed goat or turkey. There used to be a lot of turkeys on the ridge where our house was built in 1901, land that would become an elegant streetcar suburb. There were a lot of gypsies too, and so the land was alternately referred to as turkey ridge or heathen ridge. The bone sleuth said it was often customary to put bones in a hearth at the time.

It was all simply a reminder of how deeply personal our houses are, and that there are mysteries inside them. And there remain mysteries within ourselves, forgotten original surfaces, atavistic youth that we must cover and bury as we grow, but that we ignore at our peril as we age. Yes we must abandon certain dreams and goals, but not the spirit that forged them in the first place.

If your house is old, you probably have an unused chimney. Make it work. Reveal something meaningful. ⇐

Call your friends and say "I love you"

Take the advice of this Generation X journalist and novelist and reinforce your friendships now. Make sure your friends know how important they are to you at 40 and later.

by Sophfronia Scott

Sophfronia Scott wrote for *Time* and *People* magazines before publishing her novels, *All I Need to Get By* and *Unforgivable Love.* Hailed by Professor Henry Louis Gates, Jr. as potentially "one of the best writers of her generation," she currently helps entrepreneurs write books and teaches at Regis University.

Yes, I said call your friends. Don't e-mail them. Don't instant message them. CALL. If you doubt this advice or if you feel it's unnecessary because you believe you're up to date with your closest friends, then answer these questions:

- How are your friends feeling these days? The answer "fine" doesn't count!
- What challenges are they facing?

- What are they celebrating?
- Are there opportunities for you to lend them a hand?
- Who do they love?
- Do they know you love them?

I'm talking about the kind of interaction you have when someone is really, truly in your life! When you know about their dream to start a business and they know about your secret desire to open a spa on the land you bought last summer; when they know you're tired this week because you've been up three nights straight with a sick child and you know your best friend is fed up with working for a boss who she's pretty certain has a bipolar disorder. I'm talking about all that stuff that you laugh and cry over, the events, moments, people, and places you love, even though it sometimes seems so cliché after the overexposure and manipulation by Hallmark and Mastercard commercials. This is when there is a connection between people, an exchange of each other's deepest innermost selves, as well as simply the sheer enjoyment and charge you get when you're in the presence of someone you care about. When was the last time you felt that?

If you haven't felt that in a while, it's because that feeling has been lost in the glaring white ether of technology. E-mails and IMs and text messages give the wonderful illusion of being connected, but that's actually all it is — a grand illusion. And you don't even realize it until someone asks, "How's so-and-so?" and it dawns on you that you don't really know. Or you suddenly feel lonely, like no one understands you and you don't trust or understand anyone else. You've been starved emotionally and technology is the culprit. Your beloved BlackBerry is the enemy.

Why is getting reconnected (and I don't mean rebooting your computer) so important? Since I turned 40 I've felt that the number of people I know and who intimately know me is not going to get much bigger. I don't feel I will let many more people into my life at this point. It takes a different type of effort to make a friend now (that fox in *The Little Prince* was one smart critter) and I am careful whom I choose to make that effort for.

Also, I've become painfully aware of the fact that the number of people who have known me since high school or college will not grow — in fact, sadly, it has shrunk as I've lost classmates in both groups. I realize now that these relationships are precious and the types of love I feel for some of these friends can't be duplicated. For instance, I have an adoring, little sister kind of love for some of my male friends from those years. I love them truly, madly, deeply and I feel like I'm 15 or 18 or 22 whenever I'm around them. They can do no wrong in my eyes and that only comes from having seen them through the sparkling rose-colored view of youth. I suspect they also like being seen this way — they get to be eternally the football star, stage wunderkind, or brilliant young scholar — so the enjoyment of our connection is mutual.

Likewise with my female friends, our love has grown out of watching each other blossom, be vulnerable, and persevere through the cycle of decades. I have seen a friend launch herself out of a Warrior II yoga pose into a fearless new life; I have seen a classmate walk away from years in a legal career to return to her first love, filmmaking. How many more opportunities will I have to witness, connect, support, and be supported through these kinds of changes?

So call your friends, and when you do, don't forget to feel, and revel in the feelings, that forged your friendship in the first place. Feel the love — and maybe, just before you hang up, say "I love you."

Do you have to? Yes! You'll be okay; no one will get hurt or embarrassed. We're not getting into the sexual arena here. We're talking about you freely expressing what is in your heart and giving an enduring gift to your friend. I have yet to say "I love you" to a friend and not have them be surprised, delighted, touched, comforted, or encouraged. So make a list (I actually made a chart) of the people you most want to stay connected to and make a commitment to call them every other week. If that's too much for you, start off with once a month. It may sound like a lot. And I'm not talking about calling that whole list of 300 or more people you send holiday cards to each year. I mean those people who are close to your heart even when you haven't spoken in a while, and when it's been a good long while and the neglect is obvious, you're almost scared to call because you think they might be mad at you. But then a miracle happens: They call you first.

That's happened twice to me recently and I wanted to bawl my eyes out the minute I heard those familiar voices on the line. How many people would do that to you? I congratulate you if it's as many as 20, but most likely it's as few as five or six. You can make five or six calls. I know your life is busy. However, as we get older, the "busyness" will fall away. We'll leave our jobs. Our children will grow up and go off to live their own lives. The people who want stuff from you will eventually stop calling.

And then what's left? Only your relationships, those exquisite roses you have so lovingly tended with time, attention and care — hopefully. Take a few minutes now to maintain a friend. It may seem like nothing; or it may seem hard. But in a few years you'll see it meant everything. You'll be glad you took the time. Because what's left is the people you really love. ⇐

Section Two

GAIN NEW GOALS

Move mountains

This mountaineer and global traveler writes about how you can be an architect of change in the world.

by Alison Levine

Alison Levine served as team captain of the first American Women's Everest Expedition in 2002. She has climbed the highest peak on each continent and skied 100 miles across the Arctic Circle to the geographic North Pole. Levine spent two decades in the business world after completing her MBA at Duke University and left Wall Street in 2003 to serve as Deputy Finance Director for Arnold Schwarzenegger's successful campaign for governor of California. She is the author of *On the Edge* and the executive producer of a documentary, *The Glass Ceiling*.

By the time I turned 40 I had climbed peaks on every continent and had served as the team captain of the first American Women's Everest Expedition. Most of these expeditions were great and I'd come home on a high, and some of them were awful and I'd come home wondering how in God's name I had survived. I'd ask myself, "What the heck did I get from THAT experience other than a thorough ass-kicking?" But then as I would stare at my torn clothes, trashed gear, and cuts and bruises, I'd think about how cool it is to travel to these far-away countries and how much I always learned from spending a few weeks totally outside of my comfort zone.

There is nothing like third world travel to make you realize not only how lucky you are, but also how easy it is to lend a hand to others. In 2005, I was invited to join a woman named Nicole Dreon on a climbing trip to the Rwenzori Mountains in western Uganda. These mountains border Uganda and the Democratic Republic of Congo (formerly Zaire), a region that has been plagued by border conflicts for decades. Despite their beauty, the Rwenzoris were not a popular climbing or trekking destination because they are shrouded in mist 300 days a year and the region receives more than 8 feet of rain.

Once we arrived in the local village outside of Rwenzori Mountains National Park, we discovered some unsettling facts — women in this area are considered property of men and essentially have no rights and no access to jobs, education, or healthcare. The incidence of deadly disease is high and the average life expectancy is low — only 42 years. Many of the women in this village are single mothers with no access to capital. Many were turning to prostitution for income; the lucky ones moved in with their parents. The typical family home was a 10- by 10-foot mud hut with no running water or electricity. Mothers could barely feed and clothe their children and there was little or no money to send the children to school.

Working as porters or guides in the Rwenzori Mountains had always been a very lucrative job for local men, but women had never been allowed up these mountains because their culture considered it taboo. The local women were always told that the gods would be angry with them if they ventured into these peaks — the Rwenzoris had always been a man's domain. The revenue stream of the mountains was off limits to the local women.

I came to this region to climb a mountain, but I could not ignore all that confronted me upon my arrival. I wanted to help these women and determine a way for them to change their situation.

After much negotiating with the park service and the head of the village, we were granted permission to recruit women to come with us into the mountains for training in trekking-related jobs. We got Rwenzori Mountaineering Services (the organization that employs the guides and porters who work in the mountains) to agree to a deal where they would pay the women the same wage as they pay local men if the women were strong enough to make it up the mountain and back down again in one piece while carrying the standard load of 27 pounds on their backs. When we began this quest, we had no idea if any women would be interested in becoming local mountain guides. I wasn't sure my view of their situation and their view were the same.

To our surprise, seven local women showed up to meet us at the start of the trek and they all wanted to work in the mountains! Our efforts were further strengthened when the male guides and porters agreed to work side by side with us to help train these women.

Those first seven local women completed the Rwenzori trek and earned a paycheck for the very first time. They made history and paved the way for other women to start working in the mountains as well.

When I returned to the village a year later, double the number of women lined up for a job training in the mountains. I was shocked by the number of local men who came up to shake my hand and say "thank you for helping our women." I feared that they would be at least a little miffed about women having what had always traditionally been considered men's jobs in their culture, but instead these men were welcoming and supportive toward our goals and actions.

I am sure those seven women who first went with us to the mountains had no idea that their courage would have so much impact on their community — but they have now changed the way an entire culture looks at women. All they needed was someone to champion their cause and help them find their voices.

When you figure out that you can survive for weeks, months, or even longer with just the things that you can carry in your backpack — it's pretty empowering. All of the gear and belongings we carry in our packs are probably more than most Ugandans will own in a lifetime. You realize very quickly how much stuff you have that you really don't need — and you become very aware of how it can weigh you down. I think everyone should experience traveling in a developing nation. Plunge in. Meet the people. Understand what their lives are like while simplifying your own. Walk in their shoes (although most don't have any shoes, so I would encourage you to give them yours before you leave). And finally, know that you can make things happen.

The lesson I learned from the whole experience is that when we take it upon ourselves to serve as architects of change, we really can move mountains. ⇐

Seize the dreams of your youth

Advertising executive by day, musician by night, Steve Doppelt reminds you not to let your day job tie you down.

by Steve Doppelt

Steve Doppelt is a creative director and writer and is currently a Copy Director at MSNBC. Penning commercials for clients from Sprite to Budget Rent a Car, he has won awards including the Clios and the One Show. Under the alter-ego name Steven Mark, he has also put out three albums available on iTunes, Amazon, and through other retail outlets.

If someone had told me a few years ago that by my 40th birthday I'd be a singer/songwriter with three CDs under my belt and all my songs available on iTunes, I would have laughed. But now I know better. While music is a young person's business, being older provides some key advantages: the money and professional savvy to successfully record and market your work.

Sure I had grown up idolizing the likes of John Lennon, REM and Kurt Cobain. I had played guitar and sung in coffee shops all through college. But I had long ago put away my acoustic guitar for a career as an advertising copywriter and creative director. With my 40th birthday just a few years away, it seemed like my musical dreams would forever elude me.

Yet even as I began winning advertising awards and saw my career grow, I knew something was missing. Something that didn't require daily compromise. Something I could truly call my own.

So I took my guitar out of its case and began spending my nights playing the same songs I'd fooled around with in my 20s. I had never before written anything of my own. But now, with more life experience, I had a wealth of new topics to dig into, insights I couldn't have understood 20 years earlier.

After six months, I had 15 songs that weren't half bad. A friend at work suggested I make an album — she had a friend who could produce it for me. I had collaborated with this guy before on commercials, and since he lived near Woodstock — with all that town's musical gravitas — I figured I'd found a perfect fit.

I began living a double life. My weeks were all about advertising. But when Saturday morning broke, I hopped on a bus at Port Authority and headed to Woodstock, where we experimented with musical arrangements and vocal harmonies. Building songs felt familiar — not so different from editing and putting together a commercial.

After nine months. I had a fully produced, mixed and mastered album. I titled it *Distraction,* because it had been a great diversion from my day job. I used my middle name instead of my last name so I could divide my identities just as I split my time.

Somehow these divisions gave me the freedom to explore further. Now all I needed to do was market the CD. The process was mostly trial and error. I knew this was a weird time for the record business, with labels going under as MP3s replaced CDs. But I quickly saw this was also a great time for do-it-yourself artists who wanted their material to be heard.

Moreover, I now had the money and industry acumen to hire proven professionals to help me. I engaged a designer to create my Web site and MySpace pages, both essential in today's digital age. I hired a radio specialist to get my songs on triple A and college stations, and I brought in a press person to get the CD reviewed by Webzines. Most importantly, I sent my CD to a Web site called cdbaby.com, where do-it-yourself artists can sell their CDs online and get their music onto iTunes, emusic and other digital download stores.

I also hooked myself up with other new marketing sites such as Broadjam and Taxi. They give artists the opportunity to respond to industry listings and to e-mail MP3s of their music to A&R people at record labels and to music supervisors for film and television

At this point, the only thing left to do was form a band to perform in New York City. Here again my age and career experience were invaluable. I approached a commercial music company I'd worked with and they gave me names of studio musicians who also performed live as backup musicians. The guitarist, drummer, and bassist I found have not only become my live band but also my friends and the musicians and producers for two subsequent albums I produced over the last four years.

So now, as I celebrate my 40th birthday, I've recorded three albums and perform periodically at clubs in New York City. I receive monthly updates of my CD and my download sales on cdbaby and iTunes. I've even had one song placed in a small independent film.

And I've learned that your day job doesn't necessarily have to tie you down. In fact, if you use it right, your day job can actually free you up to make your other dreams come true. All the music I've made has been

funded by my job in corporate America. And what can
be more "punk rock" than that? ⇜

12

Take the entrepreneurial plunge

Owner of her own consulting firm, this entrepreneur and single mother of two writes about her experience of trading in the golden handcuffs for a life of flexibility.

by Sarah Butterworth

Sarah Butterworth is a single mother of two and was owner of a consulting business. With years of ad agency and book packaging experience under her belt, her consulting firm, ButterWorks Limited, provided services to the publishing and healthcare communications industries. In 2013 Sarah decided to start a second career in education. She currently is Assistant Head, Community Partnerships Director and Director of US Admissions at Highgate School in London, England.

I was in Vegas with my friend Seth on a Saturday night. I had just finished an all-day business meeting there, on top of a week of long hours at the agency in New York. I was miserable at work but as a 35-year-old single mother with two young daughters, I needed my pharmaceutical-marketing salary to fund my family's existence. I had always been the primary bread-winner, even during my marriage, but now, more than ever before, I felt an overwhelming sense of responsibility that urged me to persevere and to keep working hard.

In my office of about one hundred employees, mostly women in their mid-20s to mid-40s, I was the only female senior manager who had children. My daily working life involved the complete denial of my maternal role. No one asked me about my family. I did not display photographs or finger paintings in my office. I did not volunteer information about my double life. I felt like a gay man, forced to hide his sexuality in the conservative fifties. My parenthood was totally in the closet and it felt like a dirty little secret.

The daily stress of juggling the 60-hour weeks and the weekend travel for work, with the motherly tasks of baking cakes, read-alouds in my daughters' classrooms, grocery shopping, and general life administration, was taking its toll. I talked to Seth about a time in my future when my girls would be away at college and I could finally choose a profession I desired, rather than maintain my status quo in a career that I despised and an in an environment that was toxic.

Seth looked at me earnestly and said that, by his calculation that moment would arrive when I was nearing 46. But meanwhile, he wanted me to know that his own father had dropped dead of a sudden heart attack at age 45. He decried my arrogance in thinking that I had all the time in the world to live a better life. I suddenly allowed myself to think about what might happen. What if I deviated from my ten-year plan and tried to affect this seismic change sooner?

Within six months, I had left my job, with enough money in the bank to fund my lifestyle as a stay-at-home mum for the last two months of the school year. I relished being at home and able to go to the school gates to pick up my children. I loved that the mornings were no longer the hectic, crazed ordeal of the three of us walking out the door together at 7:30 AM , the kids to go to early school and me to start my work day.

My children and I then planned an extraordinary trip for the summer, with bicycles and a tent. We set off on our epic journey in late June, visiting the UK, my home country, and going on to France and Italy. The girls spent August with their father and I continued my bicycle expedition around the globe.

I took a detour to Australia where I experienced the thrill of bobbing out on the Indian Ocean in a sea kayak. From there I went to Thailand where I signed up at a cooking school, and under the tutelage of an exuberant chef, scouted the crowded Bangkok markets for fresh ingredients and learned to combine them into the perfect Tom Yum soup. Lastly, in India, I revisited the place where I'd held a volunteer job many years ago, and saw how the grass-roots medical van we used to drive around the villages had given way to a state-of-the art hospital in Sawai Madhopur.

By the time I returned in September, I felt a deep sense of relief that the loathsome memories of my twelve agency years were rapidly diminishing. But my relief was tempered by terror at the prospect of keeping my family financially afloat. My bank account balance was dwindling and I was still no closer to defining my dream profession.

I knew what I did not want to pursue but had no idea what I really wanted to do next.

Finally, I hit upon the solution: I would start my own company, take on select agency assignments on my own terms, and pursue a career in book packaging. For many years I had produced a best-selling consumer book for a major New York publisher about pharmaceutical products. My hope that my former client would allow me to bid on the project as an independent was realized, and then, eventually my proposal came out ahead.

I will never forget the feeling of excitement upon hearing the news of my successful bid. I was completely ecstatic and three years later that euphoria is still palpable. Of course there are times when work is thin, and the reality of my situation can still be overwhelming. But as I approach my 40th birthday this year, and assess my life, I so appreciate the flexibility that self-employment affords.

A couple days ago, my daughter Olivia asked if I would chaperone her class to the American Museum of Natural History. Simultaneously, my best friend Pascale invited me to celebrate her 40th birthday in London at a party, on the day after the school trip. Once, my work environment would have forced me to turn down both requests. In this new phase of my life, I can say yes if I choose to, and prioritize those very important human connections.

I no longer lead a double life and martyr myself to my job. I feel a deep sense of contentment when I realize how much more fulfilling it is to work for myself. In spite of the risk involved in owning and running my own company, the joyful freedom that it bestows is priceless.

✵13✵

Go back to work

This teacher tells her story of going backward to move forward and how she nailed her dream job.

by Tina Grant

Tina Grant left a career in social work in her late 20s, choosing to stay home and raise her children. But as she saw age 40 looming on the horizon — as she confronted the tedium of folding laundry and vacuuming dog hair — she went back to school and began pursuing her lifelong dream of teaching English. It wasn't easy: Her marriage and finances fell apart. Now with a new career and a new love, Tina knows what it means to follow your heart.

When I was 38, I started taking roller skating lessons — I suddenly felt the need to learn to skate backwards. As I struggled with the task, I realized I'd been skating backward most of my adult life. Now, at age 40, I'm about to purchase a starter home — again — and am only now entering my tenure year teaching high school English.

Some might assume that the changes I made as my 40th birthday loomed were the result of careful decision-making. In my case, however, decision would be semantically incorrect — I went on pure gut. I was compelled to make a change after spending the eve of my 35th birthday contemplating once again the unfulfilled tedium of a stay-at-home mother putting away socks and vacuuming dog hair. It's a noble, fulfilling profession for many of my friends, but I had long overstayed my welcome.

Having given up my career in social work to stay home for six years, I needed marketable skills. I wanted something that would provide intellectual stimulation and give me time with my children. Teaching had called to me since I was five years old, and I was fortunate enough to have already earned a bachelor's degree in English. So — in the midst of a separation from my husband — I applied to graduate school to secure a master's degree and teaching certification. At the same time, I was busy raising two young children.

When people ask me how I did it, I have no answer. Gumption seizes me in feverish spurts. The drive to succeed was innate — easy — but the way I got there was a lot more complicated. Half way through my first unpaid, full-time student teaching experience, my estranged husband lost his job. What little child support I had been receiving ceased. With no income, I raced through the money I had from the sale of our four-bedroom colonial, paying for tuition, rent, and groceries. As the money dwindled, the irony of my situation was palpable: I was trying to better my life with an advanced degree, yet at the same time, I found myself crying in the office of social services filling out a request for public assistance. I knew how to do it; I'd been a social worker. But here I was, going backward again, from a custom kitchen to food stamps.

I'm sure friends and family, though endlessly supportive, thought I should quit school and get a full-time job, but there was simply no way I could stop. Tenacity oiled my skates and my destination was clear. It took a long ten months before my estranged husband was employed again; in the meantime, I amassed an unenviable credit card debt and was forced to move three times, once because my young children made too much noise for my elderly neighbors, once because another neighbor threatened my children and me.

Through the tumult, I maintained a straight A average. But I also ate more than my fair share of humble pie. Being observed and critiqued by people with narrow portfolios of life experiences challenged my ego — most of my fellow graduate students were young enough to be my children. But the discrepancy in our ages actually energized my mission. It become obvious to me that age, for once, offered many advantages. Having been a professional and a mother, I had an ease in front of the classroom that some of my classmates lacked.

Now that I'm standing at the head of the class day after day, I have the joy of knowing that I've finally found my passion. And one passion has led to another — teaching has introduced me to the love of my life, a fellow teacher. The unexpected gifts of my new career add layers of contentment and ease to my life while still challenging me daily.

Maybe going backward gives me an unusual trust in my instincts; maybe I just like being different. But at 40, I'm finally able to relax and wait for the next adventure to present itself. For me, going backward is the best way to travel.

14

Stop doing things you don't enjoy

Rewrite your job description to apply your strengths at work using the steps outlined by this best-selling business writer and one of the world's leading authorities on employee productivity.

by Marcus Buckingham

Marcus Buckingham holds a master's degree in social and political science from Cambridge University. He spent 17 years at the Gallup Organization, where he conducted research into the world's best leaders, managers, and workplaces. The Gallup research later became the basis for the bestselling books *First, Break All the Rules and Now, Discover Your Strengths*, both co-authored by Buckingham. He has been the subject of in-depth profiles in *The New York Times, Fortune, Business Week*, and *Fast Company*. He now has his own company, providing strengths-based consulting, training, and e-learning. He lives in Southern California with his wife and two children.

Midlife is often a time for re-evaluation and reflection, which makes it an ideal time to listen to your gut instincts and fill your days and weeks with activities that you enjoy. Most of us are really not that far off from living the life we want and doing a job we feel good about. Follow these steps to determine your strengths and get you where you need to be.

Figure out what a strength is

By the age of 40 you need to figure out what your strengths are. In order to be able to do that, you've got to realize what the proper definition of a strength is. A strength is not necessarily what you're good at. More precisely, a strength is an activity that makes you feel strong. There are a lot of things you're good at that you have no appetite for at all. Sometimes, for whatever reason, nature blesses us with abilities, but forgot to charge those abilities with any kind of positive emotion. Any activity, whether you're good at it or not, that makes you feel strong is a strength. But beyond those activities that you're good at, there are other signs of a strength. Here's how to recognize a strength:

- A strength is an activity you look forward to doing before you do it.

- A strength is an activity at which you are completely in your zone, you find it easy to concentrate, and time goes by very quickly while you are engaged in it.

- A strength is an activity that when you complete it you are left feeling fulfilled.

If you want to find our what your strengths are, you

need to pay extraordinarily close attention to how you feel before, during, and after you do something. How you feel about specific activities will tell you what your strengths are, as well as determine how good you get at them. Your appetite will drive your ability.

Loved it or loathed it

The answers to what your strengths are lie in a regular week of life. Here's a simple way to determine those activities you're drawn to or those things you do that intrigue you and fulfill your life. Those are the things that you are meant to excel at — those are your strengths. Take a blank pad of paper. Draw a line down the middle of it and on the right-hand side write, "I loved it." On the left-hand side write, "I loathed it." Carry this pad around with you for a week. While you go through the week, if you find yourself looking forward to an activity, scribble it down in the proper column. If you find yourself completely in your zone while you're doing an activity, or if an hour's gone by without you even noticing or thinking about it, scribble down that activity. And if, when you're done with an activity, you get a fulfilled feeling, scribble that down. Do the same with your opposite reactions. If there's an activity you feel constant anxiety about before you do it, write that down in the "loathed it" column. If you work at an activity and you cannot focus on it or you have no attention span for it, add that to the proper column. If when you're done with an activity you are left feeling like an empty husk, drained, like you don't ever want to do that again, scribble that down, too.

Once you have recorded your specific activities in the loved it/loathed it columns for a week, (as you go about your day, not at the end of the day and certainly not at the end of the week) you'll end up with a distinct list of loves and a distinct list of loathes.

Clarify your strengths

Once you have done the loved it/loathed it exercise for a week and have identified at least three of your strengths, study them for the wisdom they hold. There are four questions that you should ask yourself when you look at your strengths statements. There is detailed and helpful information to be found in every strength statement.

- Does it matter why I was doing that activity?
- Does it matter who I'm doing it with?
- Does it matter when I do this activity?
- Does it matter what this activity is about?

Use the answers to these questions to rewrite and pinpoint your true strengths.

Turn the best of your job into the most of your job

Most people's jobs involve a whole range of activities — some of which they love, some of which are boring or neutral to them, and some of which drain them. Most people are not in the entirely wrong job. They're not living a second rate version of someone else's life. They're living a second rate version of their own life. Most of us have heard the call of our strengths early enough to be somewhere in the vicinity of where we want to be. We're using our strengths, most of us, at least once a week at work. But you can't win on once a week. You can't achieve anything of any significance only using your strengths once a week. You'll burn out, actually, on only once a week.

The challenge is this: On a weekly basis you have to deliberately do something to put more of your strengths into play. Determine what changes you have to make in order to fill most of your day and most of your week doing activities that invigorate you. In order to take your "loved its" from once a week to most of the time, you've got to slowly tilt the flow. You've got to build a job you really love. You've got to learn how to take your job description and recast it or sculpt it around certain activities that for no good reason other than the clash of your chromosomes invigorate the living daylights out of you. You've got to learn how to rewrite your job description under your bosses nose and get him or her to want you to do that without ever understanding what it is you're really doing.

There's risk in backing your career and your life on your strengths. But when you get to be about 40, the risk of not playing to your strengths becomes more painful than going with the flow. At 40, you've got plenty of responsibilities, perhaps even a measure of success, but your strengths are your needs. If you don't find a productive way of channeling them, they're gong to come out unproductively. Spend your days doing those activities that strengthen you. You've got to stop doing those things you don't enjoy. By turning the best of your job into most of your job, you will not only satisfy your strengths, but it will benefit your job, your team, and all those around you.

15

Be the mother of reinvention

This mother of three guides you through life-changing possibilities of an unpregnancy — the nine months you need to give birth to a new you.

by Julia Roberts

Julia Roberts is the author of *Mother of Reinvention* (Running Press) and *RV There Yet? A Cross-Country Cautionary Tale* (Book Surge). Since her first unpregnancy, she has cut a larger swath in life — performing in community theater roles, putting in a 1,300-brick patio by herself, and working to have her town build a community pool. She created the "Motherhood to Otherhood" program and started offering it in seminars in her community. Visit her at www. motherhoodtootherhood.com.

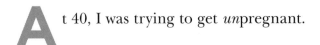

At 40, I was trying to get *un*pregnant.

This wasn't a shameful secret — my urgent desire to be *un*pregnant. I did not have a medical condition. I was trying to free myself of a mental condition — the strong, nearly undeniable urge to have a fourth child. I knew that pregnancy would be in direct conflict with my other desire — to become whoever I was destined to be...the writer, the public speaker, the comedian, the singer. I wasn't even sure yet who that was, but her name was not "Mommy."

My husband and I have three children. And they are unique and wonderful humans — each an extraordinary addition to the world. Our children are offbeat, brilliant, and funny and their future (and future impact on the world) I cannot predict. This would-be fourth child was a relic from my girlhood expectations, and not something I rationally wanted in my life.

Yet, I longed for the commitment of pregnancy. Once you accept the reality of pregnancy, you just sign up. It's a done deal. In nine months, you're going to deliver.

There are certain inevitabilities:
- Your body is going to change — and feel like something alien.
- You quit drinking (and smoking if that's another vice).
- You eat well; you drink milk.
- You get your rest.
- You take good care of yourself.
- People you hardly know touch your belly.
- People get excited and talk about your body.
- You feel good about your body — most days.
- You feel depressed about your body — most days.

Pregnancy is a very positive and exciting time. More than that, pregnancy's a learning experience. I learned to respect and admire my body. I learned to view it for more than its shape and size.

I was positive. There were no recriminations or dread, no feelings of deprivation. *Yes! You can eat!* I was entitled, because I was nourishing one of my children, but I was also nourishing *me*. And when I faltered in that right, or erred toward chocolate ice cream and a sinking feeling of low self-esteem, I had a nautical newborn to keep me on even keel.

You have express permission to nap. I didn't feel put-upon by my exercise regimen. With a small wonder in my womb, I quit working toward an unrealistic, ideal body. I merely exercised to feel better, to maintain energy, and to keep my back from aching.

Aside from a healthy perspective on your body, pregnancy offers another gift. You reconnect with family. You have a new and different relationship with your partner, your parents, your siblings, your in-laws. Even your relationship to your community is deepened.

As you progress from pregnancy to motherhood, your future dawns. You see the world beyond your generation. You feel your responsibility as a role model, protector, and champion. You are pushed to make your world better, safer, or simply happier.

As I wished for a pregnancy, it came to me in a flash: I wanted my own *rebirth*. I wanted to take the same 40 weeks and dedicate them to growing my *brainchild*. I wanted a new life that filled me with curiosity, excitement, and energy that can only be achieved from a true sense of purpose and a giddy enthusiasm.

My 40-week *un*pregnancy was my time. It was my first *un*pregnancy, so I didn't know what to expect. I had no distinct plans. I wanted merely to find out what I wanted — and not a boy or a girl.

I hoped to feel as valued and important as I did when I was carrying a child. I hoped to feel fear, mingled with awe. I hoped to find the courage to take on something bigger than myself, scarier than childbirth, and as fulfilling as becoming a mother had been.

For 40 weeks, I would be obsessed, moody, and need extra sleep. I would refuse certain invitations. I would indulge cravings. And I would deserve whatever I identified as my desire. I would be the fickle, fabled, finicky female associated with pregnancy — but secretly *un*pregnant, working toward some new me.

Every mother knows how dramatically her life can change in 40 weeks. We've done it before. And so, I started. Steadily, I lost 50 pounds, as if I were merely coming back to myself. I reconnected lovingly with my husband, on a cruise for his 40th birthday. I spent time with my children to redecorate their bedrooms to reflect their own creativity and spirits. And I began to write the book based on my first *un*pregnancy: *Mother of Reinvention.* I assembled moms in *un*pregnancy groups to help them craft their own unpregnancy experiences. We began to see what a life-affirming and powerful model for achievement pregnancy had been in all of our lives. Unpregnancy gave us each a roadmap to transformation. (By comparison, sports metaphors such as "go for it!" or "Score!", were meaningless.)

In each of our lives, and collectively, pregnancy is a crucible. It is the business of our species. It presses its way on to our life lists, and takes priority on our agendas. Whether we start early, procrastinate, or keep our planned pregnancies right on track, pregnancy gets itself done, born, checked off. And so I came to understand, as a mother of three, that pregnancy was the most productive model in my life for how to succeed, persist, insist; in short, how to get things accomplished.

As pregnancy had once reshaped my thoughts, actions, and intention, now *un*pregnancy accomplished the same end. Over time, *un*pregnancy became the mother of my reinvention. ⇐

16

Bounce back at 40

After reflecting on his midlife to-do list,
this fitness expert writes of finding a renewed
sense of purpose in an old career.

by Christopher Blake Mays

Fitness expert Christopher Blake Mays is certified with the Aerobics & Fitness Association of America (AFFA) in Step, Katami, Bosu, and Rebounding and is the Group Fitness Manager of Equinox in New York City. He had a weekly video blog on iVillage.com called "The Week in Celeb Fitness" and has been featured in *The New York Times, Fit Magazine, Spa Magazine, Child Magazine,* and *Good Housekeeping* as a fitness expert.

'll admit it: I was frantic about turning 40. Truthfully, what bothered me the most was the fact that it bothered me so much. I had no good reason for wanting to be 39 forever. I was in great shape and was the regular recipient of comments such as, "But you don't look like you're about to turn 40." But that didn't matter — I felt 40. Or I felt what I feared 40 to be, lethargic and outdated. To my surprise, I fell victim to all the clichéd uncertainties that come with approaching that age, and even though knew it, I just didn't know how to set in motion any of the equally clichéd remedies to get myself over it. Many people turn to exercise to help them through this period in their lives, but that would do me no good. I had exercised and taught classes almost every day for the past umpteen years. My renewed sense of purpose would have to come from somewhere else — or so I thought.

I tend to be pretty hard on people when they walk around feeling sorry for themselves, so I'm pleased to say it didn't take long before I pointed the finger in my own direction. I knew I was numb, robotically going through my activities, so I snapped myself out of it by listing the things I had always wanted to do.

My list didn't end up being very long: 1. Write a book. That was as far as I got. The thought alone felt good. I hadn't written much since graduate school and I had never written something just for myself, so I was curious to see what my stories and insights would look like spilled out across a page.

I wasn't sure what form the book would take, but I knew I wanted it to be a guide on how to align your mind, body, and spiritual being. On paper I was qualified to give such advice even though I wasn't feeling very physically and mentally united myself. This self-assigned project helped a little though. Each page was a new beginning at the end of every day. As the project started to take shape, I found myself writing my own athletic history. I told of the many types of classes I had taught and the experience of teaching them. I told of the reactions I got from participants, and I told of the physical feats I witnessed in many of them.

People had come to me with different goals — some wanting to lose weight, some wanting to tone up, some wanting to bulk up, all wanting different versions of themselves. I felt it only fair to tell my future readers about the one class where I had seen the greatest improvement in the most people — rebounding. It was a class I had taught for years, but after a recent job switch from Crunch to being the Fitness Director at a new club called Club H, I found myself teaching it more often. I've seen many people get very nervous before this class (more so than any other class), to the point where they couldn't get enough of it. Not only have I seen bodies change with rebounding but attitudes as well.

Rebounding is an exercise that takes place on a mini trampoline. People tend to be nervous about trying it because they don't want to suffer the embarrassment of falling off. Unlike jumping on a regular trampoline, the aim with rebounding on a mini trampoline isn't to bounce high, but to perform a series of small, controlled movements. The trampoline absorbs 80 percent of the body shock so it's not as jarring to your joints as floor exercises, and the movements help lengthen your muscles, creating more of a dancer-type body due to gravity, acceleration, and deceleration. I find it also helps detox your body; it increases the collagen production (which aids in looking younger) and helps decrease varicose veins. The effect is not just psychological; the action of bouncing up and down against gravity stimulates the lymphatic system without trauma to the musculoskeletal system.

As I said, I had rebounded countless times before, but I had never written about it. Knowing that I wanted to include the feats of rebounding in my book I started paying closer attention. The exercise experience became brand-new as I tried to note all of my movements and emotions while paying special attention to those taking the class so I could head home and record everything accurately. I also researched more of the benefits. I discovered that it assists in the rehabilitation of heart problems; it improves resting metabolic rate so that more calories are burned for hours after exercise; and that it also allows for deeper and easier relaxation and sleep. I had known this all along and couldn't believe that I had let myself slip into so much of a routine that such a stimulating exercise went unnoticed. I started teaching more rebounding classes and sharing all of the health benefits with members before class. I found myself becoming not only a rebounding advocate, but also a life advocate again. I felt a physical resurgence and renewed purpose. In other words, I bounced back.

My updated enthusiasm for class started to spread. New people came in all the time telling me they heard about how great rebounding was from this person or that one who had taken my class. A woman who works for iVillage.com approached me one day after class. Our chat led to my becoming an on-air personality for the site doing "The Week in Celeb Fitness" commentary. Writing my own script each week eventually led to writing fitness articles for the site as well.

Now, I am very much enjoying combining an old career with a new pursuit. The book is still a work in progress — as am I. The moral of the story is: This dog learned to re-like an old trick.

Section Three

HEALTH AND FITNESS

17

Get strong

An exercise physiologist explains how to let
fitness fuel a heightened sense of power.

by Lisa Hoffman

Lisa Hoffman, MA, is an exercise physiologist and owner of Solo
Fitness (solofitness.com) who creates exercise programs that are
tailored to the needs of midlife women. She is the creator of Make
a PACT for Life!® , one of the industry's first physical activity
and education programs for cancer survivors during all stages of
treatment and survivorship. Also she is the author of two books:
Better Than Ever, The 4 Week Workout Program for Women Over 40
and *The Healing Power of Movement: How to Benefit from Physical
Activity During Your Cancer Treatment.*

B elieve that the fitness program that best meets
the specific needs of women older than 40 is one
that focuses on weight-bearing and strength-building
exercises. If "weight-bearing" sounds too serious, don't
worry; it can be as simple as taking a walk through
the park or doing a 20-minute exercise session to your
favorite music.

I see the years from 40 onward as a time when women

deserve to enjoy a heightened sense of power, wisdom, independence, and self-acceptance. It's a time that can be turning point — one that inspires you to start and stay with a fitness program that makes you feel better than ever, retaining all the strength, energy and confidence you need to enjoy an active and satisfying future.

One of the key things to consider right now is strength training. After nearly two decades of focusing on the benefits of aerobic exercise, fitness professionals are now encouraging strength training for women. For women in their 40s, there are a number of compelling reasons to add strength training to their weekly routines. Foremost is the need to strengthen the muscles attached to the bones to help prevent or manage osteoporosis and reduce the risk of fracture. Strength training also can reduce the risk of back problems and injuries; and it can help you lose fat, firm your body, and improve your figure. And, according to some experts, it can even offset some of the symptoms of aging.

It's a sad but true fact of life that many women find their waists thickening and their bodies becoming less toned as they age. Strength training, along with healthy nutrition, is a primary way to counteract the dreaded "middle age spread."

There's an expression I use to motivate clients: you *have to lift weight to lose weight*. To be more specific, while strength training may not lead to weight loss on the scale, it's likely to result in fat loss and a slimmer appearance.

Lose Fat and Build Muscle

Strength training will help you shape your body into the shape you want. The loss of body fat and increase in lean muscle tissue can noticeably enhance the way you look and feel. After a few months of regular weight training, you may notice that your stomach is flatter and your waist is more defined. Your breasts may appear firmer and higher as the underlying pectoral muscles become stronger. Indeed, your entire body can become firmer and tighter.

Strength training workouts also rev up your metabolic rate which means you'll burn more calories during all activities, even sleeping. In their 40s, most women begin to lose muscle, and for every pound of muscle lost, your resting metabolic rate drops by nearly 50 calories a day. This process can be reversed as your metabolic rate rises when you build muscle.

Posture and Presence

Strength training can also improve your posture, which has a powerful influence on how others perceive us and on how we feel about ourselves. A slumped posture can cause a woman to look and feel insignificant, weak, and lethargic. An uplifted posture says to the world: Here I am, proud and powerful! Mature women with beautiful posture are noticed, respected, and admired.

But many women who want to improve their posture just don't have the muscle to maintain it. Good posture requires strength — to keep your spine elongated, shoulders down, and back and neck long. Strength training gives you the muscle to maintain elegantly erect posture.

The significance of posture goes beyond appearance. Posture affects your energy level, since it can either restrict or facilitate blood flow. Good posture also reduces your risk of headaches, backaches, and painful spinal misalignments.

Positive Power

During their 40s many women achieve new levels of power in their professional lives. With strength training, you can match and fuel your professional power with an exciting surge pf physical power. Here's what some women have said about their muscle strength work.

"Getting strong has made me more secure and confident in so many different areas of my life. It's great not to feel weak and helpless anymore."

"Strength training helps me cope with so many everyday things — carrying groceries, cleaning my house, everything!"

"I do a lot of business traveling, and now that I'm stronger, I enjoy being able to handle my own luggage easily.

I always book hotels that have gyms."

"Strength training makes me feel stronger mentally as well as physically. I feel more powerful and confident when I'm negotiating a business deal."

The Definition of Strength Training

Many people, however, confuse strength training with body-building or weight-lifting. These sports are actually advanced or extreme forms of strength training and far different from the typical strength training exercises I recommend.

Strength training, which also is called muscle strength/ endurance exercise, involves working individual muscle groups. This can be done by using your own body weight as resistance, or an outside force such as weights, bands, tubes, water, or equipment in health clubs.

There are three basic forms of strength training: isotonic exercises, which are typically performed by raising or lowering a weight through a joints full range of motion (typically done with free weights or machines such as Nautilus or Universal); isometric exercises, which involve contracting the muscle and holding it in position for a few seconds; and isokinetic exercises, which are usually done on equipment that uses a hydraulic form of resistance (generally in clinical or rehab settings).

The routine I advocate combines a basic warm-up with a

series of strength-training exercises and a cool-down in four easy-to-follow routines. If you do it two days a week (with at least one day of rest between each session), you can be assured your program is balanced and safe.

If you keep at it, you'll find that a strength training program will firm and tone your body. You'll notice development in your shoulders, arms and legs, a firming of your abdomen, buttocks, thighs and other subtle changes. You will *not* develop large bulky muscles from doing strength training alone.

As with any fitness routine, check with your doctor first, and work with qualified trainer who respects your body's limitations. And remember: A midlife woman's power comes from her mind, not just her muscles.

18

Defy your age

Instead of being more cautious with your emotional and physical self, this yoga master encourages you to push your heart and body to take on greater challenges.

by Edward Vilga

Edward Vilga is an accomplished writer/director and one of New York City's leading yoga teachers. A Yale graduate, he is creator of a series of best-selling yoga books and DVDs that have been translated into seven languages. Vilga has eight books published, ranging from academic texts to mass-market best sellers. His course for DailyOM (3M subscribers) *A Year to Get Rich With Purpose* reached #1. That course currently has more than 21,000 students enrolled.

Last month, my local optical chain refused to sell me another box of contact lenses since more than a year had passed since my eyes were last checked. I can't remember the last time my prescription changed — and I've been wearing contacts for at least 20 years — but I knew there was no way around the 15-minute exam. Sure enough, I learned that my eyes were exactly the same as they were two years ago. At the end of the exam, however, the well-intentioned Vision Care Specialist shocked me by warning that I would probably soon be needing reading glasses. "It's just something that happens when you get to be around your age." She began explaining things further, giving some reasons why this was part and parcel of reaching the advanced age of 43. Motivated by professional kindness, her demeanor nonetheless revealed her certainty that my physical decline was not only inevitable, but also well underway.

Eight years ago, when I was a mere 35, my life more or less fell apart. A long-term relationship ended suddenly and violently, resulting in tremendous personal and financial chaos at a pivotal moment in my career. For a long-time, I felt like I was sleepwalking.

Growing up, I was your classic bookish malcontent, prowling my way through my local library, desperately searching for some kind of meaning in my adolescent life. (Even now it's rather frightening to think that if I were born a decade or two later, I might have wound up a goth.) Instead, I gained a smattering of library book-based knowledge about psychology, philosophy, and even the occult, lingering a bit longer on whatever seemed more esoteric and exotic (and therefore, I assumed, more likely to be helpful toward surviving suburbia). And so, somewhere in my early teens, I devoured my first books about yoga.

In spite of myself, I was a reluctant, latent athlete, able to try (and sometimes succeed) at the strange poses I saw in Swami Vishnudevananda's *Complete Illustrated Book of Yoga*. But drawn as I was as an adolescent to yoga, I never began a steady, consistent physical practice. It wasn't the time.

But then at 35, it was. With my life unraveled, wandering through my gritty hipster Manhattan gym, I stumbled into a yoga class. I'm not sure why I chose to attend — probably just a whimsical desire to contrast my regular traditional workout. In fact, I'm pretty sure I sauntered in with the class already in progress.

I remember being sore the next day, particularly in my thighs. And I remember being shocked about that, given that I was a runner and lived in a fifth-floor walk-up. Because or in spite of that, I came back to another class. And then another. And then another after that.

Soon I discovered the teachers who suited me best — the most challenging ones, but with either a sense of humor or irony — no granola, cool-aide drinkers for me. And I found one in particular, a yogic Janis Joplin, whose energy and enthusiasm I found totally electrifying.

Within two years, I was enrolled in teacher training, not really so much intending to become a teacher, but more because I was hooked on the rush and intensity of my own yoga practice. Now, more or less a yoga junkie, forever on the hunt for the next yogic high and physical challenge, I needed to go deeper. I craved more mystic thrills.

I've always been able to do a pose referred to as "Wheel Pose" — in Sanskrit, *Urdhva Dhanurasana.* Basically, you lie down on the floor, bend your knees and plant your feet. Reaching your hands besides your ears, you press down, straighten your arms, and lift everything besides your hands and feet off the ground. The body takes on a big bow shape, resulting in a major back-bend.

There are several different kinds of potential obstacles to achieving the pose. For some women, it's an arm strength issue, while for other muscular guys, the shoulders are too tight to allow the arms to straighten enough. For people of both genders, however, often the obstacle is more psychological: opening the energetic heart-center of the body this way simply feels too emotionally vulnerable.

While I could always do a decent wheel, no matter what emotional issues I might be having, the daredevil in me became fascinated with a virtuoso variation called "Dropping Back." Standing, one simply falls backward into wheel pose. It's only there that capital F Fear met me head-on.

You learn dropping back first by being assisted in the falling backward motion. In other words, you are "dropped back." The first person who dropped me back was my Janis Joplin instructor. The instructor faces you, his or her leg between yours, framing your hips and back as they dip you backward. The move has a feeling of a tango-like dip to it. They are supporting you in a vital and intimate way, and you are trusting them not to let you crash to the ground and bust open your head.

Being dropped back by a yoga teacher you trust completely has an element of risk and excitement to it, but it's nothing compared to dropping back on your own. You are falling backwards, trusting that somehow the floor will be there and that your arms will support you. Logically, you know that both your arms and the floor can generally be counted on . . . but still that open-hearted backward plunge is terrifying.

In fact, it was only as I neared 40 that I found myself ready to attempt it. I knew the floor was solid. I knew my arms were strong. But I didn't trust something — I didn't know what exactly — or maybe I just didn't trust enough, period. I could never do it without the assist.

And then it started happening. At first, very awkward, leaning more to one side than the other. Many times, I'd lightly bang my head on the way down. I got better at it, despite lots of rocky, awkward splats. Extensive practicing, and more and more information about backbending in general helped, too, I suppose. But honestly, I mostly learned how to just let it happen, knowing that I'd come up on the other side OK.

And after a year or two of wavering and wobbling, I'd pretty much gotten the knack of it — able to pretty much drop back whenever I was sufficiently warmed-up enough. Like a handful of other difficult poses — my party tricks as it were — I had it down.

I'm not sure where or when, but I somehow heard about a hard-core practice that particularly intrigued me: dropping back on one's birthday . . . as many times as you had years to be thankful for! By this point, in a single class, I'd dropped myself back two or three times. And every now and then in class my favorite teacher would bring me up and down rapidly four or five times or even six times, always assisted by her infallible support.

But only when I turned 41, was I ready and able to make the attempt on my own. Forty-one falls backward into the void.

Frankly, there's not much to tell other than that I did it. Yes, I was drenched with sweat. Yes, I nearly conked myself out a few times in the mid-20s and 30s (talk about a metaphor!), but I did it. And I was extremely pleased with myself.

Now we all know that yoga is supposed to be non-competitive, even with oneself. Yet nonetheless, I'm not bothered by my pride in achieving this. I could do something that once frightened me (that frightens everyone). Something beyond the range of 95 percent of my fellow students in their 20s and 30s. And I could do it 41 times.

And the following year, I did it 42 times. And then this past year 43. And in three months, I will be doing it 44 times. I'd like to think that when I'm 60 or 70, 80 or 90, I'll still be able to drop back once for each year I've lived.

I can't help but sound a little boastful, but I didn't make up this tradition — although I wish I had. Beyond the tremendous exhilaration and physical openness it creates, I also really like the "Fuck You" toward aging.

Rather than taking it easy and slipping quietly into that good night, try raising the bar one notch higher every year. Indeed, the older you are, the more opportunities you've had to develop fearlessness, more chances to trust that you can fall backward open-hearted and catch yourself. God knows, I didn't really know that when I was 35 and adrift. I certainly didn't have a clue in my 20s. It took me 40 years to trust enough to even attempt falling backward on my own.

And so when the Vision Care Specialist, in the nicest possible way, cautioned me that my eyesight — make that my entire body — was degenerating moment by moment, year by year, and that there was nothing I could do about it but comparison-shop for bifocals, I could only smile.

There was no way she could know that I was in fact, getting more flexible, and more importantly, more fearless with every year. After all, she was at best 32. Give her time . . .

19

Use a midlife crisis to transform yourself

Stop waiting. This physical therapist implores you to discover ways to shift your perceptions, interactions, and behaviors now to take advantage of these high-energy years.

by Lisa Sattler

Lisa Sattler PT, DPT, MS is director and owner of Midtown East Physical Therapy and Rehabilitation Services of Astoria, LLC. She is founder of the Treatment Center for Repetitive Strain Injuries. She has 25 years experience working in the physical therapy profession with the last 17 years dedicated to neck, shoulder, and arm pain syndromes. She has lectured nationally and internationally and her treatment program has been published in Dr. Emil Pascarelli's new book *The Complete Guide to RSI*.

Midlife crises are underrated for their transformative powers. In fact, I have found it valuable to allow my intermittent midlife crises to spark my energy and motivation, and move me into new areas of growth.

When a midlife crisis strikes, you'll know because you'll

start to feel energy building, and that energy needs to go somewhere. If you try to contain it, it can turn into anxiety. Channel that energy instead into something good. Use your professional and personal experiences to create a new mindset.

By the time I was 40, I was comfortably established in my career with a private practice in physical therapy that was profiting and gaining speed. It would have been easy to let life fly by, missing out on years of experiences by working a lot, albeit doing something I love.

I count myself fortunate to work with injured people. It feels good to make a positive contribution. It's also beneficial to come to work and forget about my "problems" as I listen to patients describe their own pain and struggles.

Because I specialize in upper extremity pain syndromes, I see many people injured from working on their computers or playing musical instruments — repetitive motion injuries. Most have been very seriously injured so they begin treatment with constant pain. Some cannot brush their teeth, open a door, or wash their hair without extreme pain and/or the tingling that precedes numbness. Knowing that there is a long path ahead for many of them, I am happy to be able to take part in their healing.

My physical therapy practice has helped shape my ability to transform my approach to life in my 40s. Here are some of the ways I recommend using your midlife angst to motivate you to transform yours:

1. **Cultivate the art of staying in the moment.** Most of us live in our heads — in the past or the future, remembering things we did yesterday and thinking about how we could have done them better, or thinking about what to do later, or tomorrow. The only thing that is real is the present moment. Some eastern teachings suggest that the purpose of pain is to bring people into the moment.

2. **Use the moment to become a better listener and deepen your relationships.** At work, I find my ability to recall details from one patient session to another has improved about 70 percent since concentrating on this approach.

3. **Practice putting 100 percent effort into what you are doing, in the moment.** I have realized that when I do this, the future unfolds naturally, and the effort becomes the reason for my overall success.

4. **Find ways to enjoy life.** I can create happiness for myself most days simply by reminding myself of my good health and that of my immediate family and friends. I encourage the patients, as they slowly improve, to look

inside themselves for the way to this path. It's even more of a challenge to be happy when you have pain.

5. Try to avoid the routine rut. We set up patterns of behavior to make it easier to get through the day without having to make constant decisions. Routines help us to be efficient; it helps to have a plan. But at this stage of life, decisions are getting easier. Jar yourself out of some of your rote ways of doing things and leave yourself open to new solutions.

6. Create periodic "vacations" by using a new technique to steer away from stressful events. Don't wait until you get to the point where you find yourself saying "I need a vacation." Once you do, it's already too late.

Instead, try saying "I need a midlife crisis." With the midlife crisis as the engine, you can affect change in your life, and you have the potential to create real relief from stress. The changes that result from redirecting that energy can transform your days in ways that don't disappear, as the relaxation typically does, when you return from a two-week vacation.

7. Find a way to feel that you have a purpose. Volunteer at a charity or shelter doing something meaningful for someone else. Surround yourself with positive, optimistic people who share similar goals.

8. Use exercise to enhance your quality of life. Taking care of yourself better physically — your body and your skin — will pay back in this decade and over the years.

I found weight training twice a week very valuable for improving my outlook as well as my shape. I've discovered periodic facials and regular home face skin care using eye creams and moisturizers help slow the unfolding of fine lines and wrinkles and help me feel better mentally.

9. Do all those things you've always wanted to do. Go scuba diving, take a dance class, spend a little extra money on yourself. Be a good example of how to have fun. Explore how to motivate yourself with a midlife crisis to do something daring you've dreamed of.

10. Stop worrying about what other people think. It's a trap that can stifle creativity and blunt your ability to discover what you're good at. Don't let outside opinion inhibit you anymore.

When I was 37 my mother passed away. She was only 59 and she was convinced she was going to live to be 80. This experience shifted my thinking about life and I realized I wanted to "live" life, not just wake up, go to work, get through the day, go home, and start over.

I felt some energy start to build when I was 39, and in evaluating things, I realized having a child was a significant life experience I did not want to miss. I was 41 when I finally had a successful in-vitro fertilization — against many odds. My daughter's birth has helped me to feel more a part of life, and happier than I ever imagined.

The way I see it, by the time we reach 40, we have a limited number of years of high energy left to really make things happen. It's important to remember that the years have always been limited. Now they are just more limited. So stop waiting.

20

Give lifelong care to the skin you're in

Taking care of your skin is a lifelong concern. Dr. Beer reminds you that it should top the list of medical precautions on your midlife list.

by Kenneth Beer, MD

Kenneth Robert Beer, MD, specializes in cosmetic dermatology and skin cancer surgery and is a founder and director of "Cosmetic Boot Camp" — the leading training seminar for cosmetic dermatologists. He received his medical degree from the University of Pennsylvania, his dermatology residency and dermatopathology fellowship at the University of Chicago, and holds a faculty appointment in dermatology at Duke University. His private practice is in West Palm Beach, Florida.

My experience of turning 40 was probably atypical because I am not a huge milestone person or terrifically sentimental. I do, however, think that 40 is a milestone in that one transitions from any vestigial remnants of early adulthood to being a grownup (as opposed to being a kid with a grownup house and job). As a physician, my biggest concern really was that I was crossing the threshold into middle age and that I would now have to confront issues with my own health and mortality as well as those of my parents. I like to be in control and didn't want a lot of health issues catching me off guard. I wanted to make sure the biggest surprise of turning 40 was the party my wife threw for me in Palm Beach.

The concerns centered around my health because I realized that 40 is a time when things start to go wrong. Accordingly, I got a stress test, colonscopy, and an MRI to try to eliminate any of the easy things that can kill you. It is said for men that turning 40 ends the fear of testicular cancer and now enables you to worry about your prostate. However, I was worried about the smoldering things such as diabetes and cholesterol, and I got tested thoroughly for those.

When patients ask me what their midlife regimen should look like, I have a rehearsed response. I recommend that one should exercise for at least 30 minutes per day to increase cardiovascular health and that at 40 one should seriously evaluate one's diet. Also, if you smoke, 40 is a great time to stop — smoking is obviously awful for your insides and it makes wrinkles worse.

One of the best things you can do at 40 is look at your family tree to see what genetic weaknesses you may have. If, for example, all your relatives die from heart attacks at age 43 or get colon cancer, then you should discuss your specific risks for these with your physician. If you have a physician that either does not know how to deal with these issues or does not care, you should consult with one who does. Buy yourself a great 40th birthday gift — a physical with a doctor who is thorough.

As with all other precautions that should be taken around the age of 40, skin care needs to be at the top of the list. When patients inquire specifically about skin care at 40, I paraphrase Kurt Vonnegut — sunscreen. If you don't listen to anything else about skincare, use sunscreen. It has been shown to decrease the risk of several types of skin cancer and it will help fight wrinkles. Truth be known, most skin damage occurs before the age of 25, but additional insults after that age don't help matters. I tell my patients who are 40 or older to go out and enjoy life but to avoid getting sunburns and use sunscreen, and yes, I do follow this advice myself. There are dermatologists who recommend living like a hermit and who follow their own advice. I think that is foolish.

There are many, many things one can do to help reverse skin damage after 40. One can use antioxidants, which include green tea and coffee berry among others. One can get treated with lasers to stimulate new collagen production. One can also wear polarized sunglasses;

they decrease your risk for macular degeneration and minimize wrinkles.

I know it gets a bad wrap in the media, but Botox is the most effective anti-aging procedure on the market, and I think the numbers bear this out. More than 3.3 million people are getting Botox treatments every year. This procedure stands out because it is low-risk and effective, and people are typically quite pleased with their results. Fillers would be a close second because they can help erase creases such as smile lines. There are also many topical products that help reverse aging of the skin (including Retin A), and I encourage people to try to reverse the damage. The skin is a dynamic organ and it is capable of repair.

There are certainly people who ask if wrinkles are a natural part of the aging process and should be left alone. To them I say, I make my living fighting skin cancer and wrinkles, but I don't push people to fight wrinkles unless they want to. If they want to embrace their lines and, as some say, wear them like a badge of courage, that is fine. If they want to get treated with lasers and Botox and fillers and cosmeceuticals, that is fine, too. Again, I am pragmatic, so I think that whatever the person chooses to do, it is my job to help them do it.

Some people tend to anticipate the day when they no

longer have to worry about their skin, but that day won't come. Skin care can be a big problem for infants (who have large surface to volume ratios and can get all kinds of skin problems); it's an issue for teens, when acne and breakouts can lead to low self esteem and depression; and it can be just as bad for adults when melanomas begin to take their toll. Having healthy skin really is critical at all parts of life — the same as having a healthy liver or lungs or heart. Just as with any other vital organ, care of the skin is a lifelong concern. ⇙

21

Stop stressing out

This Buddhist practitioner invites you to make peace your default setting with mindful meditation.

by Diana Winston

Diana Winston is the Director of Mindfulness Education at UCLA's Mindful Awareness Research Center at the Semel Institute of Neuroscience and Human Behavior. A nationally known Buddhist teacher and member of the Teacher's Council at Spirit Rock Meditation Center, she founded the Buddhist Alliance for Social Engagement, an urban Buddhist Peace Corps.

One glance at friends and colleagues, all amazed we 've finally hit 40, reveals a common characteristic. Whether we're climbing the career ladder, coasting from our successes, juggling the eight million mommy/daddy responsibilities, awash in cash or debt, or contemplating that proverbial red sports car — we're all stressed out.

Much of my adult life has sent me in search of an antidote to stress — mental, physical, and existential. At 22, I could barely make sense of my post-college life; I was so lost in confusion and discontent. Who was I supposed to be in the world? What would bring me happiness?

I thought India might hold some answers, and after a month of so of tourist attractions and beach towns I stumbled upon a meditation retreat in the foothills of the Himalayas. On a whim, I imagined that Buddhist mindfulness meditation practice could make a difference. Little did I know it would be the start of the next 18 years of my life.

Mindfulness is about bringing attention into the present moment. It's about being with things exactly as they are with a kind and non-judgmental attention. We humans tend to be lost in thought: planning, worrying, remembering, judging, hating ourselves or others, or comparing ourselves to everyone around us. Mindfulness can remind us that if we take a breath, relax, and gently bring our attention into the present, we can find ease and well-being. We can find freedom from stress, at least for that moment.

For a driven, anxious, outer-directed, and somewhat self-critical young adult, mindfulness was the balm I needed. I meditated for months in retreat centers and throughout Asia. I spent a year in the forests of Burma where I shaved my head, donned peach-colored Buddhist nun's robes, and committed to a vow of silence. Hour after hour, alone in my hut, I devoted myself to bringing my attention back to the present moment, trying to wake myself up from self-centeredness and disconnection.

I wanted a life free of stress. I wanted to stop the endless seeking outside myself for my happiness. I saw that in each moment I was mindful, I was free from my mental stories. I discovered that happiness wasn't dependent upon external conditions. Instead, living a life that was connected to myself — where I could slow down, contemplate, check in with what was true, and allow my own innate wisdom to emerge — was what brought a life free from stress.

Science has shown that mindfulness meditation can impact the physical health of our immune and nervous systems; our mental health by regulating moods, helping with anxiety and depression; and it can improve our focus and attention. Cutting-edge research shows that mindful awareness can actually impact the brain. Brain scans of long-term meditators reveal a thicker prefrontal cortex, the part of the brain responsible for flexible thinking, self-knowledge, emotional regulation, and empathy.

Currently, I work at UCLA where I teach mindfulness at the Semel Institute for Neuroscience. We're bringing mindfulness out into the public sphere and sharing the science behind it. From the Buddhist monasteries straight to Los Angeles, we're introducing mindfulness to a city much in need of de-stressing.

We've seen how amazing this simple practice is — stop, breathe, be aware, check into yourself, let go of what's disturbing you, and come into the present. The science is showing that you really can transform your mind. You can find peace inside yourself, even in the midst of the busy, chaotic, stressful lives we lead in this century. In a culture that tells us that happiness is external, that we have to strive madly to reach our goals, and that stress is inevitable, mindfulness is revolutionary.

Of course I still struggle — finding ease is the result of lifetime practice. Sure I get annoyed in the midst of traffic or overwhelmed by the amount of e-mail demanding attention. But it doesn't usually last that long; the turn-around time is faster. When I get lost and disconnected, the internal reminder to return to the present moment emerges from deep within me and invites me to stop and breathe. And peace becomes more and more commonplace — my default setting.

So I invite you to spend some time at 40 getting mindful. You can take a class or read a book to learn the practice in some depth. You can start immediately, exactly where you are, whether you're driving down the freeway, separating your squabbling children, composing that long-avoided e-mail, or reading this. Stop now, take a breath, and notice how you're feeling and what you're thinking. What is the truth of this moment? Feel your body, alive and present. Breathe. At 40 we're not getting any younger. This is your life. It would be a shame to miss it.

Have a heart-to-heart
with your parents

Are you prepared for a family medical emergency?
Dr. Rabkin encourages you to understand and
document your parents' choices now.

by Miriam Rabkin, MD

Miriam Rabkin, MD, has worked in the field of HIV/AIDS for
20 years, focusing on strengthening health systems to improve the
delivery of prevention, care and treatment services for underserved
populations. She is an Associate Clinical Professor of Medicine
and Epidemiology at Mailman School of Public Health, where
her clinical practice focuses on strengthening health systems,
improving access to HIV services in resource-limited settings, and
the design, delivery, and evaluation of chronic care programs for
HIV and non-communicable diseases.

Many people reaching age 40 are moving into a
caretaker role for their parents or grandparents.
In addition to assisting with doctor's visits and medi-
cines, there is a "big picture" area where your help can
be invaluable — the creation of "advance directives"
that assist physicians in providing the care and sup-

port that is best for each patient. We doctors look for advance directives — living wills, health care proxies, and "do not resuscitate" orders — to guide the care we provide at the end of life.

Talking to elderly relatives about advance directives can help them tell their physicians about the type of end-of-life care they would prefer. Tips include:

- Talk early: Don't wait for a crisis. Asking questions in advance helps the family explore issues and provides the opportunity to have discussions with physicians, friends, and clergy.

- Be specific: What is the question you are trying to answer? Is it, "who will make decisions?" or "what decisions should be made?"

- Use examples: Specific examples make it easier to discuss end-of-life care. Whether you are talking about Terry Schiavo or great-aunt Mary, parents can say, "That's the kind of care I'd like," or, "Don't let that happen to me."

- Involve your parent's doctor: If he or she doesn't raise the subject, you should. Clinicians will be able to explain a parent's prognosis, the types of decisions that are most likely to occur, and the specific forms used by the hospital, city or state.

- Document decisions: As with all estate planning, advance directives should be documented and witnessed. A lawyer may be helpful but is not required. Health care providers can explain which forms to use, and most American hospitals have ethics committees and patient relations departments if additional help is needed.

Ideally, people will consider end-of-life care while they are alert and aware, in a setting unconstrained by finances, family pressures, pain, or time. As long as individuals have what physicians call "decisional capacity" and what lawyers call "competence," their choices are all that matters. They can ask for care to be withheld or withdrawn or sustained as they see fit — even if others think it is a bad idea.

But what happens if people cannot participate in medical decision making? If they are unconscious? Demented? The next best person is a health care proxy — someone chosen in advance to step in and make decisions in the event that the patient no longer can. He or she explains what the patient would have wanted.

If a patient does not have decisional capacity and does not have a health care proxy, health care providers will try to find someone else who knows what the patient might have wanted — most often the patient's spouse, sibling, or adult child. These surrogate decision-makers can participate in medical decision-making, but some states restrict the types of decisions they can make.

Most physicians, lawyers, and patient advocates recommend that the elderly or seriously ill have, at the very least, a formal health care proxy. Designating a proxy and making sure that person knows the patient's feelings about end-of-life care is the best way to preserve both power and flexibility.

Planning ahead: parents who can decide

- Choosing a proxy: If a parent can participate in this type of conversation, it is a good place to start. Of course, the proxy must understand what your parent wants. Some people have strong feelings about blood transfusion, artificial nutrition, or mechanical life support. Others have more general philosophies — "If I am in a coma and the doctors say I'll never recover, I don't want to be kept alive by machines." It is important to realize that there is no right answer and no single approach to end-of-life care. It is also important to know that advance directives are not set in stone. If your mother changes her mind, she can change her advance directives.

- Writing a living will: These allow elders with specific wishes about health care to spell out their intentions, philosophies, and preferences. Often drawn up by lawyers, they give the health care team insight into the kind of treatment the patient would want. Rarely, however, are living wills able to anticipate every eventuality, so it's a good idea to have a health care proxy as well.

- Requesting Do Not Resuscitate (DNR) orders: In the United States, health care professionals (including EMS) will resuscitate almost everyone unless they have a DNR order. Since CPR cannot cure an underlying disease, and is rarely effective in the very old or the very ill, many older patients would prefer that it not be attempted.

Planning ahead: parents who can't decide:

- Choosing a surrogate: If your parent is unable to have these discussions, and there is no proxy or living will, physicians will work with a health care surrogate, ideally a spouse or adult child familiar with the patient's health and medical issues.

- Planning ahead with the health care team: Once a surrogate has been chosen, he or she should talk to the health care team and indicate the preferred course of action. If you think your parent would have wanted a DNR order, say so. When it comes to advance directives, there is no substitute for informed participation.

If you are caring for an elderly or ill parent, don't be afraid to plan ahead! Parents usually welcome the opportunity to talk to their loved ones and doctors about their philosophy of health care, their goals, and their preferences. You do not need to make every decision in advance, but educating yourself and your parents about the options is an important first step.

23

Take a swing at golf

Whether you're starting now or you're already golfing,
this LPGA golfer reminds you that you'll be able
to play the game for another 40 years.

by Michelle McGann

Michelle McGann has won eight LPGA tournament titles. She was
heralded as the next great women's player when she first qualified
for the LPGA tour at the age of 18. Despite a diagnosis of juvenile
diabetes, she recorded five top-10 finishes in her third season on
tour, and has since continued as a championship player. With her
colorful shirts and trademark hats, Michelle is also active in the
Diabetes Research Institute and a founder of the Michelle McGann
Golf Classic, benefiting the Diabetes Research Institute.

I started playing golf when I was eight — my dad was a
terrific athlete and I loved spending time with him in
the Florida sunshine. He was a great teacher, and by the
time I was 30, I'd won seven LPGA tournament titles. It
wasn't always easy, though. I'd contracted diabetes and
suffered an eye injury that required three surgeries and
gave me double vision for a while. But my love of golf
kept me coming back to the game, and I found ways to

counter and overcome the physical difficulties I faced.

Now, as I begin to see age 40 coming up on the horizon, I recognize all golf offers people that age. You're on a beautiful course, getting fresh air and great exercise. You're competing, meeting new people, and strengthening established friendships. You'll be able to play the game for another 40 or 50 years. And if you want to get a leg up on your career, you can certainly do that. I play with CEOs and I'm amazed by the amount of business that goes on. More and more women are joining these professional/amateur events, seeing how much fun it can be to mix business and pleasure.

Keep it simple is the advice I give people interested in getting started. You don't have to spend a lot of money to test your interest in the game. You don't have to be in top shape right away, either — you can be a terrific competitor without doing all that running around you see on the tennis courts. And no matter what level you reach, you can enjoy the beautiful lawns and landscapes of private clubs and public courses.

The first thing you need to do is line up a good instructor. Your stance, grip, and swing are all extremely important, so don't try to teach yourself these basics. If you belong to a club, you can find a good instructor there. If not, ask friends: Word of mouth is the best way to identify someone with the right skills and experience.

Invest in a couple of clubs. The equipment can be pricey so don't spring for a full set until you know you're committed to the game. A nine-iron and a putter are a good start, and as you continue you can also acquire a pitching wedge, a seven-iron or maybe some type of wood. There are a lot of beginner sets, and it's best to get an LPGA or PGA professional to help you select from among them.

Pay attention to dress codes. Things have loosened up quite a bit over the last several years, but golf is still a game where personal style matters. Being conservative may mean wearing bright clothes that make a strong style statement! But khakis are always fine at private clubs and so are T-shirts with collars. Some places require that women wear skirts, though shorts are usually fine now. Call ahead if you're not sure, and remember that public courses can have dress requirements, too — you're unlikely to see anyone there dressed in a bright pink tube top.

Keep a grip on your confidence! We all play because we love to compete, and one of the biggest things that will aid your success in golf is your state of mind. You can hit a string of great shots and think no one can beat you — and then you hit a couple of bad shots and your confidence goes down the drain. When I started playing, we didn't have mental coaches and psychologists helping us; we had to find our own ways to lift ourselves out of the downward spirals. You have to learn to clear your head, visualize those terrific shots you were making, and bring that level of skill back to the situation at hand.

Golf can be a frustrating sport — it's you and the ball and nothing else. If you're a good athlete, you want to do everything right, but that perfect shot in golf doesn't come very often. Then too, there are the days when it's windy and raining. You think, maybe that desk job isn't so bad after all.

But golf has a pull; it brings people back. There are always frustrations: There were times when I was leading a golf tournament; then all of a sudden my blood sugar would drop to nothing. Other people face other kinds of obstacles. But you go back and give the game the best you've got. It's terrific to have a sport that keeps bringing out the best in you like that and rewards you in so many ways.

24

Obsess and reassess

Writer Jonathan Ames faces his obsession with physical disintegration and catalogs his ruination.

by Jonathan Ames

Jonathan Ames is the author of *I Pass Like Night*, *The Extra Man*, *What's Not to Love?*, *My Less Than Secret Life*, *Wake Up, Sir!*, *I Love You More Than You Know*, and a graphic novel entitled *The Alcoholic*, illustrated by Dean Haspiel, and published by DC Comics. Jonathan Ames was the winner of a Guggenheim Fellowship. He is also the creator of two television shows: the HBO series *Bored to Death* and the STARZ series *Blunt Talk*. His novel *The Extra Man* was made into a film starring Kevin Kline, and *You Were Never Really Here* has also been adapted for the screen, starring Joaquin Phoenix.

I'm 41 years old, and I'm absolutely falling apart. I'll start from the top and work my way down, cataloging, as it were, my disintegration.

I am bald, except for the sides of my head. All the stuff at the top has just about melted away. There are a few resilient, aberrant strands, so I buzz my hair down with clippers so that I don't look like I have mange.

My eyes, from staring at a computer all day, are often blurry and in pain. I bought reading glasses a few years ago, but they are so smudged that I think they are making my eyes worse. I shouldn't stare at the computer so much, but I'm addicted to Internet backgammon and I'm a writer, which means I spend my days writing e-mails. The collective word count of all my e-mails would surely equal Tolstoy's *War and Peace*.

Inside my head, behind my eyes and beneath my bald dome, is a lingering mild depression, which causes me to procrastinate and not do simple tasks like cleaning my reading glasses or to begin important tasks like writing my version of *War and Peace*. Generally speaking, my depression manifests itself as this feeling of subtle displacement from my life. I'm reminded of this line from the movie *The Red Shoes*: "Life rushes by, time rushes by, but the Red Shoes go on dancing forever." All of that applies to me, except for the red shoes part. Everything seems to be rushing by, and I'm floating above it all, reaching my hand out to life, but not quite grasping it, like waving your hand for a taxi that is clearly occupied.

My nose gives me a lot of trouble. When I was 5 years old, I was attacked by a disturbed youth, and he broke my small, just-forming beak. This did something to a vein inside my nose and ever since I've had hundreds, if not thousands, of nosebleeds. This past winter, my nosebleeds were the worst they've ever been. The heating in my apartment baked the interior of my nostrils, and I had two or three nosebleeds a day. I thought of going to a blood bank and hooking up my nose to some kind of contraption and earning some extra cash. Naturally, I exacerbate the situation with the occasional unconscious exploration of my nostrils with a digit (i.e., finger), while nervously playing Internet backgammon. There's nothing more humiliating than bleeding on your laptop from nose-picking while wasting time playing Internet backgammon.

Of all my body parts, my mouth is in pretty good shape. Not having dental insurance, I haven't been to a dentist in years, but I bought a tooth scraper in a drugstore and take great pleasure in removing my own plaque and tartar, which sounds like the name of a law firm. Just this morning I spent at least 15 minutes on my plaque, and I'm always amazed how quickly it comes back. It's sort of like my massive credit card bills. Every month I pay them and I experience this naive sense of satisfaction that this will be the last time I ever have to do that again. But there they are the next month. Plaque and debt are clearly spiritual brothers. One area of concern in my mouth is my front right tooth. It is half fake and completely yellow but rapidly moving toward brown. I fell in a bathtub when I was 6 and chipped my tooth, and the cap hasn't been replaced in 21 years. But this tooth gives me character; it is kind of like a mood ring, growing darker each year as I grow increasingly strange.

My neck is no good. I can't turn my head when I parallel park. I'm like the Seabiscuit jockey, who didn't let people know he was half blind. I don't let people know that I can't actually turn my head.

My right shoulder was pulverized by my enormous 19-year-old son. He still likes to have "tickle-time," though now it's called "Let's wrestle," which means that he attacks me without warning and injures me terribly. I'm kind of like Inspector Clouseau and he's Kato, and except in this instance Kato weighs 200 pounds, is 6 foot 1, and combines his Oedipal complex with a passion for weightlifting. One of my son's attacks — he sprang from behind a door and threw me to the ground, while giggling — is the cause of my shoulder problem. I've been unable to fully extend my right arm over my head ever since. Oddly enough, it's also very painful for me to reach across my body and retrieve my wallet from a sport-coat pocket. So an act that previously had been symbolically painful (see above reference to massive credit card debt) is now literally hurtful.

Recently, I got health insurance for the first time in years, and so I decided to see a doctor about my shoulder. The fellow spent about one minute with me and pronounced that I have either tendinitis or a torn rotator cuff. It's unclear. I was sent for physical therapy, which I greatly enjoyed. It was kind of like a gym for hypochondriacs. I told the physical therapist about the chair I sat in to do my e-mail writing — an old wooden chair I found on the street 12 years ago — and he said it was damaging my neck *and* my shoulder. So I purchased an inexpensive office chair. I sat in it for a day, and my lower back went numb. The physical therapist said this was because I hadn't sat properly in a chair for years. Anyway, my shoulder still doesn't work, and my lower back is still numb, but I like my chair because it has wheels.

In the last six months, I have had three precancerous moles removed from my right shoulder, middle back, and abdomen. I've received over a dozen stitches. The hole in my abdomen, like something out of a Kafka story, has not healed, and I'm procrastinating about going back to the doctor. Surely it's not normal to have a hole in one's abdomen going on four months now. These precancerous moles were caused by my childhood summers at the Jersey shore. Back in the early 1970s, sunblock wasn't widely used, and every summer I was burnt alive and would spend our weeklong beach vacation stuck to the sheets of my motel bed, which has always made me sympathetic to the abandoned wife in the *Heartbreak Kid* when I see it on the classic movie channel every five years.

Not long ago, after playing a marathon game of Wiffle ball with my son, a strange lump formed in the palm of my right hand. I noticed the lump the next day when I ran my hand over my bald head and in some weird sensory mistake thought that the lump — a brain tumor?!? — was on the skull. I looked in the mirror at my head, didn't see any tumor, and then looked at my hand and saw a lump the size of a marble. Something about the way I grabbed the plastic Wiffle-ball bat must have inflamed the sensitive tendons in my hand. It's a painful lump, and it announces itself when I grasp the steering wheel while parallel parking. The benefit, though, of this palm-lump pain is that it distracts me temporarily from my neck pain.

My stomach is actually good these days. In 2001, I had irritable bowel syndrome brought on by heartbreak and was seriously thinking of getting fitted for a diaper. I was a walking scatological time bomb. But my heart healed and my intestines followed suit. My libido is down by about 40 percent, but this is probably a blessing, though my weakened sex drive may be linked to the existential displacement described above.

The lower third of my body, I have to say, is also in excellent shape, except that my right ankle is frozen and probably in the early stages of arthritis, but debilitation-wise it's nothing to write home about. Not yet anyway.
Well, I've run out of body parts, and I'm rather relieved. If I had any more depressing limbs or organs to discuss, I might not have been able to finish writing this catalogue of my ruination. I have noted that my disintegration, like some kind of spreading tree rot, has only reached my ribs, where the Kafka-esque hole is. I don't think there's anything I can do to stop this rot

from spreading further, but at least I can watch its progress, as I might watch the lengthening of a shadow at the end of the day as light fades and darkness predominates. ⇜

Section Four

MASTER YOUR MONEY

25

Enough already — get ready for retirement!

Financial planner Mike Falcon counsels you to begin saving and behaving so you can make the big break.

by Michael Falcon

Michael Falcon was managing director and head of the Retirement Group at Merrill Lynch until 2012. Serving more than 30,000 businesses and 6 million individuals, Merrill Lynch is committed to helping people prepare for, transition to, and live in retirement. Falcon currently serves as the CEO of Asia Pacific for Global Investment Management at J.P. Morgan Asset Management Limited and J.P. Morgan Investment Management Inc.

You're 40 — congratulations! Now it's time to act your age and start saving for retirement!

Maybe, in your 20s, you thought you couldn't afford to save — I used to say I was investing in my career. In my 30s, I was starting a family and buying a house. It's easy to figure, "I've got that 401(k) going. That's enough."

But it isn't. We really do have to save. Starting now.

I know you have a vision of your retirement — dreams of how you will live. Our research at Merrill Lynch shows you probably plan to wind down a little by your late 50s. Maybe you'll change careers, teach, or start a small business. You're hoping to work part time, or on your own schedule — spending January and February someplace warm.

That's the New Retirement, with 10 to 12 years transitioning from traditional work to traditional rest — what we call the "Longevity Bonus." However, it's your financial behavior this decade — starting right now — that holds the key to how you spend this bonus of a lifetime.

Now, I don't know how much you've saved already, but the odds are not very much. And while you have plenty of good income earning years left, the truth is, the money you save in the next 10 years is the most important. Why? Because while saving in your 50s and 60s will help, there's a lot less time for that money to compound. A dollar at age 40 can grow to almost six dollars by age 70, but the same dollar at age 60 may only double. Hey, doubling is OK, but how much better would you feel knowing your savings have increased six-fold!

Being financially prepared for retirement has surprisingly little to do with investing. Oh, investing matters, but that's the easy part. The hard part is saving.

Saving also means S T O P   B O R R O W I N G !

You cannot borrow and save at the same time. It is impossible. You can borrow and invest (generally not recommended), but saving and borrowing are opposites. To save, you will need to spend less than you earn. You knew that; it's common sense. But now you need to start doing it. If you're like most of us, it will take serious change — after all, spending is usually more fun.

It is very hard to stop spending because spending is habit forming. One of the laws of inertia — the one that says a body in motion tends to stay in motion — sustains your momentum at the point of sale. But if you spend a few minutes setting your savings plan in motion, you can actually use the same law of inertia to your advantage.

The key is to G E T   S T A R T E D .

First, start with a plan. Simple is fine. I started by writing down what I earned, spent, and owed. Then I wrote down when I planned to transition, retire, and how much money I thought I'd spend once I did. Everyone's different, so you'll need to find the equation that works for you.

Next, get advice. Professional money management is essential. But you also need advice in figuring out how much money you'll need, and on managing your debt and spending. Plenty of help is available on the Internet, in books, and through advisors. In my case, since I have a degree in finance, a career in finance, and lead a multi-billion dollar retirement business…I use a Merrill Lynch Financial Advisor. Everyone needs advice. Everyone.

People who have a plan and work with an advisor are 2.5 times as likely to be saving regularly for retirement.

So, how do you know if you're getting good advice?

You know this answer. Gut-check. If it sounds like "how to beat the market fast," move on. Get advice from reputable sources that are focused on saving rates, asset diversification, and long-term performance. Successful saving and investing behaviors are repetitive, slow, and boring. Avoid fast-acting, exciting ideas. They may be fun at first, but they can break your heart and pound your wallet.

Finally, you save. So how do you find the money?

C'mon. Do I need to do the mocha-latte-a-day math-thing where you pack your lunch, iron your shirts, and have a million dollars when social security kicks in? You're 40 years old. Unfortunately, you will not find money to save by watching a new 50-inch flat panel TV. You need to have a budget and stick to it.

It's about behavior. And since we all tend to misbehave, I suggest automating good savings behaviors whenever possible. Maximize contributions to your company's retirement programs and sign up for auto-increases, so when you get a raise you save more. Use payroll deductions to contribute to an IRA and fund taxable investment accounts. Save it before you spend it.

Once you're saving, you can start investing. It's simple: diversify, asset allocate, and re-balance.

Briefly, diversify means own a variety of securities so you minimize reliance on any single investment. Asset allocation means owning different types of investments, like stocks and bonds. Re-balancing means periodically re-diversifying and re-allocating to reduce investments that have grown in value and adding to those that are now smaller as a percent of the total. These three steps will help you manage both risk and return.

Remember, you need to manage risk, not avoid it. Being overly conservative can leave you just as short on time and money as being too aggressive.

So it's that simple: diversify, asset allocate, and re-balance. Any place where you invest — your 401(k) provider, a brokerage firm, a mutual fund company — should be helping you with all of these. If not, go somewhere else.

Welcome to 40 — think about that retirement dream and start saving for it. Better yet, start behaving for it.

26

Protect the best years of your life

You probably own life insurance, but do you use it to the fullest? This top-producing agent guides you through what you need to know.

by Angelia Shay

Angelia Shay was a top-producing agent at the New York Life Insurance Company. Based in Richmond, Virginia, her designations include Chartered Financial Consultant, Chartered Life Underwriter, Life Underwriter Training Council Fellow, and Financial Adviser appointee through Eagle Strategies, New York Life's investment advisor division. In 2005 and 2007, she was named Agent of the Year by New York Life, Richmond General Office. Currently she is a Financial Adviser with Eagle Strategies LLC, a Registered Investment Adviser, and is the founder and President of THE PATH Financial Strategies.

At age 40, people have very different financial needs. Many have found their footing as professionals. Others are changing careers, going back to school, or re-entering the workforce after raising a family. Forty year olds may be single, married, divorced, or partnered; high-, low-, or middle- income earners. Some have children in the nursery; others are already facing college bills.

But there is one product virtually every 40-something can benefit from: life insurance. You probably own it already. But do you have the policy that's best for you? And are you aware of the many functions life insurance can play? One client of mine, a 42-year-old doctor who'd gone through a bitter divorce, found several months later that he had an opportunity to buy a partner out at his practice. The only problem was, the divorce had left him illiquid. When I told him he could borrow money from his whole life policy, he was thrilled! He had forgotten about the cash accumulation value.

Family Matters

If you have children or a spouse who relies on your income, it is essential to financially protect them in the event something happens to you. Is it less important to ensure a stay-at-home parent? Many couples cover both spouses regardless of their earnings because they recognize the considerable cost involved in hiring someone to provide the work a stay-at-home spouse provides.

Adequate life insurance is also critical if you're divorced and have children — it ensures the continuation of child support and other payments that depend on future earnings. At the time of divorce, you and your former spouse should reassess your coverage. If you had joint ownership of a policy, you may decide to split it into individual policies and change beneficiaries.

Even if you're single and without children, you should ascertain whether you have people who depend on you. Life insurance can replace services you provide or cover final expenses and outstanding debts.

Personal Projects

If you've been thinking about purchasing a new or second home, launching a business, or expanding the business you own, some life insurance policies can help guarantee a loan. Homeowners can choose an individual life insurance policy (instead of purchasing one through the bank) to satisfy mortgage requirements while retaining control of the policy. Likewise, some kinds of insurance make it easier to borrow business capital, because policies can help settle outstanding debts should a business owner pass before his or her loan is repaid in full. And it is worth mentioning that with the U.S. savings rate lower than at any time in history, whole life can be used to create a discipline around personal savings.

After Your 40s: Looking Down the Road

Let's assume that you and your spouse or partner both move past the transitional 40s into a secure retirement you can enjoy together — for many, the best years of life. Life insurance can help protect the estate you've accumulated. For one thing, knowing that one of you will receive an influx of cash down the road allows you to spend more of your money now. In addition, life insurance can help ensure that your estate or business will one day be passed directly to your children and grandchildren, or to a business successor, rather than being liquidated to pay potential estate taxes.

Permanent or Term Life?

As you select life insurance, one of your first decisions is whether to choose a term policy or permanent life. They both afford solid protection but have very different attributes.

- Term is the most basic kind of life insurance. It typically provides affordable protection for a predefined period of time, so it is often used to serve temporary protection needs. If the insured should die while the policy is in force, the face amount is paid to the named beneficiary. At the end of the premium guarantee period, the insured can renew the coverage and in some cases, convert the policy to a more permanent policy. Otherwise, coverage expires.

Term life is more limited than permanent insurance in the advantages it can provide. Term cannot be used to guarantee a loan, for example. Its primary benefits are affordability and portability. The premium for term life insurance is initially lower than a comparable permanent insurance policy. This initial lower premium usually makes term insurance an ideal choice for individuals with a temporary need for insurance protection. It does become more expensive as you get older, however. As needs change, the policyholder can usually convert coverage to permanent life insurance, though this becomes more expensive as the policyholder ages.

- Permanent or whole life insurance provides ongoing protection from the day you purchase the policy until the day you die, as long as you pay the premiums. When you pass, the company will pay your beneficiaries the death benefit, usually the face amount of the policy. One feature to consider when purchasing a policy is the potential to earn dividends, though this benefit is not guaranteed.

There are many different types of whole life insurance available with a number of options. Among its benefits are:

- Permanent protection that can never be canceled as long as you pay your premiums

- A level premium that is guaranteed never to increase

- A guaranteed death benefit, generally free from federal income tax

- Tax-deferred cash value accumulation

- Though not guaranteed, the potential to earn dividends

An insurer can also waive insurance payments if the insured is disabled and unable to work for longer than six months. A few years ago a client for whom I'd written whole life about ten years earlier called to say he was very sick. He'd been out of work for some time and could not pay his premiums. His family was under a great deal of financial stress. We completed the paperwork to put his two policies on waiver, something we're able to do if the insured is out of work for six months or more. This freed up more than a hundred dollars a month, and he was also able to borrow money from the contract to pay several nuisance bills.

Reassess and Remember

This is the time to think through the insurance you'll need into the future. After all, premiums are based on age and the current state of your health. Purchasing or maintaining coverage now will protect your insurability regardless of any future health problems while keeping the cost of coverage in check.

27

Open doors.
Change the world.
Volunteer.

As partner in a wealth management firm,
Brian Walsh knows that it's not what you get;
it's what you give.

by Brian Walsh

Brian Walsh was a partner at Highmount Capital, a boutique investment and wealth management firm that delivers value-added solutions to clients in three areas: investment advice, wealth management, and family governance. Highmount also places a special focus on strategic philanthropy, helping prepare the next generation of clients for the privileges and responsibilities of wealth. He recently became Managing Director at Boston Financial Management, LLC.

Most of us spend our 20s and 30s focused on the basics — gaining an education, building a career, establishing a family. It's not until you reach age 40 that you feel like you've laid a foundation and have time to breathe! For me, an important aspect of reaching that age was giving something back to the community.

I am by no means alone in this regard. We see a strong interest in community service among clients at Highmount Capital, the wealth management company where I am a partner. In additional to providing high-performing investment options, we counsel families in strategic philanthropy and community service, helping parents and their children get involved with strong not-for-profit organizations. As you turn 40, here are some pointers to help you gain all you can from your service to the community.

Choosing an organization:
Give some thought to the kind of group you want to assist. My point of entry into volunteering was my church, joining my parish finance council. It made a lot of sense for me to get involved with an organization I already knew, one that touched my family and me so closely. But other people have different priorities. Maybe you want to bring art into your life and get involved with a museum. Perhaps you care deeply about the environment and want to start protecting a piece of wilderness. Or maybe you want to take up activities that fight hunger or disease in a distant continent. The more you respect the organization and its mission, the more rewarding you're likely to find your work there.

Understanding how you'll contribute:

"Time, talent, or treasure" — those are the three things not-for-profits look for in volunteers. I also now serve on the Boys and Girls Club of Boston's Board of Overseers and can assure you from that vantage point that not-for-profits are delighted to receive any of the big three! People who don't have overwhelming obligations at work or at home can donate stretches of time to help an organization fulfill its mission. Other people have special skills to enrich the group. A lawyer, for example, can provide free legal guidance. Other people prefer to support their passion for the organization's cause with financial donations. (Or, they attract other donors who make contributions.) Time, talent, and treasure all have a critical place in strong not-for-profit organizations and all are very welcome.

Thinking about the work you'll do:

In all likelihood, your organization is going to want you to perform specific tasks — anything from organizing an auction to washing cars. Becoming part of my parish finance council was great for me — because of my professional background I didn't need any time to come up the learning curve. Other people, however, volunteer precisely because they want to broaden their world and learn new skills. As you consider joining an organization, think about the specific services you want to provide, and make sure that's something the organization needs.

Making savvy financial donations:

Donations to charitable organizations may be tax deductible with respect to income. If you're donating a significant amount of money, however, it may make sense to put your checkbook away and instead donate stock that's grown significantly in value since you purchased it. There are limits to the tax implications, however, so discuss this with your financial advisor. For significant donations, you may also want to consider split-interest trusts or other charitable vehicles.

Involving the children:

We think this makes very good sense. Children today are growing up in a time of tremendous wealth, and many of them will be inheriting large sums of money. Often, these kids have no idea how well their parents are doing. At Highmount Capital, we think it's important to help young people frame the next generation's attitudes about money, how to handle it wisely, how to invest it, how to make informed donations to charity. You don't want to show the family balance sheet to a teenager, but you can use volunteering as an opportunity to talk about how fortunate you are and how important it is to share — both your financial assets and your time.

There are many reasons to reach out and volunteer:
You broaden your circle of friends, take on new challenges, and perhaps expand your professional network, too. Of course, the biggest reward is making a difference in people's lives. Winston Churchill once said that you make a living by what you get; you make a life by what you give. I couldn't agree more.

28

Make art a part of your life

This journalist and correspondent for the art world recommends that you to forget stocks and bonds. These days, art and antiques have claimed their rightful rank as the premier new asset class, with soaring values attracting a slew of first-time investors.

by Brook S. Mason

Brook Mason is an award-winning journalist who covers the art market and colleting for the *Financial Times* and *Art & Antiques*. She serves as U.S. correspondent for *The Art Newspaper*. She is the first journalist in 55 years to attend the prestigious Attingham Summer School in Britain for museum curators and architects.

Having reached your fifth decade, you've lived through your sometimes-turbulent 20s and 30s and have now, most likely, settled into a career. Chances are, you've also bunked into a long-term abode, a place way beyond your first or second transitional home, and with that kind of new-found security, have both the time and the funds to afford and explore artful objects of lasting value. Plus, you're about to become fully cognizant of the enormous return that can be reaped from savvy investments.

And talk about stratospheric growth! Simply consider a Rothko painting selling at auction for more than 7,200 times its original value (the seller, banker David Rockefeller paid less than $10,000 for it back in 1960). With financial returns like that, no wonder hordes of hedge funders splurge on art and antiques at the drop of a hat.

But there are other, more emotional kinds of returns involved in collecting. For one thing, in owning art you sign on to a far wider community. In this fast-paced age, when communication zooms along at nanosecond speed, friendships formed over art can be as enduring as the art itself.

Yes, the eighteenth-century Chinese export porcelain tea cup I bought at age 30, for little more than chump change, may see like paltry fare. But since that time, I've met reams of people from top tier Americana collectors, to specialty dealers and auction house experts, to more ordinary appreciators of antiques, all of whom own examples of eighteenth-century Chinese export ware. We all share a bond: a passion for the period porcelain that the tea cup represents.

Now, in my 40s, having honed my eye and my own expertise, I find I've completely shifted gears. Rather than hankering after yet another eighteenth-century memento, I'm zeroing in on a totally different aesthetic, one that mirrors the twentieth century, the time period in which I've lived most of my life. Now it's industrial photography, images of factories and steel mills shot for *Fortune* and other pioneering magazines, that captivates me. Call such black and white snaps vestiges of industrial archeology.

Before you begin to collect in earnest, however, you'll need a few tools to understand the fast-paced market, track the price shifts, and buy knowledgeably. So take a tip from art world insiders and head to artnet.com, the art world's answer to the brokerage houses' stock tip sheets. Its database is the most comprehensive archive of past auction sale results: Within a fingertip's reach you'll find more than 2.9 million results from more than 500 auction houses since 1985. And added to that are gallery sale records.

While there's a nominal fee for usage, simply plug in the artist's name and up comes his prices. Even antiques are listed. Plus, there are upward of 1,500 galleries internationally on that site, so scroll those virtual showrooms. So what particular areas of the art world spanning thousands of years and cultures should a 40-something woman or fellow zero in on, cherish, and build into a budding, but serious, collection today? Plenty.

Target up-and-coming niche specialties:
With Rothkos like David Rockefeller's, and Old Masters paintings, and eighteenth century French furniture already established and pricey, savvy collectors should go after up-and-coming niche specialties. One way to do this is to go after smaller works by already recognized artists. While a massive table by Japanese-American designer George Nakashima can go for big bucks, smaller Nakashima examples (like lamps and chairs) can be had for significantly less.

Go for works that are still undervalued:
Do this by zeroing in on still affordable contenders working in a similar aesthetic. Consider the lesser known leaders of the studio craft movement, advises Bob Aibel, who runs the Philadelphia Moderne Gallery. For example, he recommends targeting the furniture of Wharton Esherick and Phil Powell, both contemporaries and neighbors of Nakashima, and whose work has been picked up by museums and twentieth-century design buffs. Or take a look at the work of the late Manhattan designer Karl Springer, who produced furniture covered in exotic skins of python, alligator, and tortoise, as well as parchment, for the likes of Frank Sinatra and Jackie O.

Watch what the museums collect:

Where museums go, collectors follow. One area is contemporary Japanese ceramics as more American museums are buying in the Japanese niche area (more than 25 museums, including the hipster Museum of Modern Art in Manhattan and the Chicago Art Institute have contemporary Japanese ceramics in their holdings). Dealer Joan Mirviss points out the ceramics of Suzuki Osamu, whose abstract forms inspired by nature and traditional shapes like jars and clay tomb figures are more sculpture than lowly pots. Beatrice Chang who runs Dai Ichi Arts, Ltd., recommends the wood fired stoneware of Yasuhiro Kohara.

Go for "name" period jewelry:

In the fast-paced auction world, Cartier, Bulgari, Tiffany, and Van Cleef are more than purveyors of major bling: They've got blue-chip status as collectibles. Consider two similar 1925 diamond Art Deco bracelets, explains Daphne Lignon, Christie's New York Senior Vice President who mans their jewelry department. The one with the Cartier name would go for nearly a third more.

Plus, remember that "period" doesn't only mean the 1920s and 1930s: Lignon recommends snapping up 1960s and 1970s jewelry. A few years back, David Webb and Van Cleef jewelry dating from those decades, barely registered on the auction scene. So watch for pieces from that period — David Webb earrings and abstract geometric gold jewelry from the English designer Kutchinsky. And men's jewelry, too — a Cartier mother-of-pearl and pearl tuxedo dress set of cuff links with matching buttons is attracting attention in the salesrooms.

Follow the vintage ready-to-wear:
"Of course, Chanel, Dior, and Balenciaga couture frocks offer steady value but ready-to-wear is also now appearing on the auction scene," says Pat Frost, Christie's London textile and fashion expert. Examples: a 1966 Yves St. Laurent Rive Gauche pinstripe pants suit, or 1970s Ossie Clark dresses. Handbags are also rocking the auction scene. "Of course, the Hermes Kelly bag is top dog," says Frost, but what's new is that Prada, Celine, and Tods are appearing at auction. "The appearance of later brands means a good buy doesn't have to be really vintage in age," says Frost. Condition, condition, condition: That's what matters in period fashion.

With advice like that, girls (and guys) can shop, shop, shop — but, even more important, bring home an investment-worthy haul.

Section Five

THE SUBSTANCE OF STYLE

29

Throw a fabulous party

Party planner to the stars, David Tutera shows
you how to plan a magnificent event in a special
place to mark your 40th year.

by David Tutera

Leading Wedding & Entertaining Expert, David Tutera is the
host of WE tv's show, My Fair Wedding with David Tutera
and David Tutera's CELEBrations. Honored by *Life & Style
Magazine* as "Best Celebrity Wedding Planner," and has an
impressive client list for weddings and events including Jennifer
Lopez, Matthew McConaughey, Elton John, Vice-President
Gore, Kenneth Cole, Tommy Hilfiger, and many others. Tutera
is the author of several entertaining books.

Plan a celebration, large or small, with the people
who mean the most to you, in a location that is
special — in this country or abroad, or even right in
your own backyard. Create an occasion that will leave
your guests with everlasting memories.

Approaching the age of 40 was an exciting time in my
life. Everything seemed to be operating at an amazing

level — from business to personal life. I realized how lucky I was to have so many close family members and friends, and I wanted to bring them all together to relish a happening that reflected my abilities and what I love to do. After throwing lavish parties for my clients for more than 20 years all over the world, I decided to give myself the gift of the birthday bash of my dreams — in Tuscany, Italy.

Since I was asking my guests to make a long trip, I wanted to give them more than just one event. I planned three days of parties and shopping. I wanted to create an experience that most of the people in my life had not had before.

I wondered how many of my friends and family would actually take the journey to Italy, and as I began to work things out, I was amazed at the number who embraced the invitation fully. When I saw how excited everyone was to celebrate this way, I took my own advice (I've often made such recommendations in my books) and made an effort to step back and enjoy the entire planning process. I am fortunate to have traveled to Tuscany several times with my partner on vacations. We love Italy so much that we had decided to return there every summer. In fact, it was a vacation there with our moms that gave me the idea to hold my parties there. The idea was to celebrate in a place that holds a special place in my heart with all the people who hold a special place in my heart.

Upon arrival, guests were asked to go poolside for hors d'oeuvres of Prosecco and Parmesan. The excitement that everyone exuded was immediate gratification for me and proof that all my planning was worth it.

After cocktails, we went into the wine cellar, which I had set up for a wonderful Italian meal, accompanied by a local trio for live instrumental music. I gave a toast in which I went around the room and said something special about each person. I concluded with an explanation for the small angel pin on each place card: It symbolized that all the special people in my life are my angels.

The following day, I transported everyone by bus for a full day of shopping and sight seeing in Siena concluding with an outdoor casual dinner of pasta and Chianti in the piazza. Everyone had acquired a wonderful summer glow. We all casually visited and dined, as if the entire piazza was my own backyard.

The final night's celebration was at a twelfth-century castle on the largest vineyard in Tuscany that has been in continuous use. I asked all my guests to dress in summer whites, and I accented all-white decorations with simple white flowers and feathers. The cocktail portion of the evening took place outside, overlooking the vineyard. Dinner and dancing were in the courtyard, under the stars and sky. Music floated down from overhead: Opera singers sang from a balcony as guests came to dine and resumed periodically during the dinner. Later, there was a DJ and dancing under the stars.

Just before the grand cake was brought out, my partner gave a toast and asked guests to step outside to view a spectacular fireworks show — in all white, of course. This night was filled with laughter and tears and love and emotion — a shared experience that none of us will ever forget.

Although a celebration in Tuscany may not be for everyone, there are ways to have such special times closer to home. What makes a celebration unique is to bring together the people who mean the most to you and give them a very personal event to commemorate it.

Remember to touch all five senses to create a meaningful and memorable experience. Capture the imagination of your guests. Entice them in a way that invests them in fulfilling the purpose of the celebration and demonstrates why it's special to you. You want to leave your guests understanding the meaning of "You."

A great party can be held in any place that has meaning for you — in Colorado or Vermont for skiing, on a beach or a boat, or even at Walt Disney World. Your friends and family will love celebrating with you because you have gone to the trouble to make your big birthday out of the ordinary. ⇐

30

Do yourself (and the world) a favor: learn to live with less

An innovative designer suggests paring down and editing your life to the most beautiful and worthy essentials.

by Harry Allen

Harry Allen is an award-winning industrial designer whose work is featured in the permanent collection of the Museum of Modern Art in New York City, the Brooklyn Museum of Art, and the Denver Museum of Art. Mr. Allen achieved prominence in 1994 for his interior design of Moss, a design gallery in New York. In the world of product design, his clients include Target, Umbra, Magis, Aveda, Ikea, and Steuben.

We are born with nothing, but that changes quickly. Baby blankets, rattles, clothes, and toys are the beginning of an accumulation process that in our modern, overabundant world never stops. It took me 40 years to learn how to edit my life down to the most beautiful essentials. And in doing so, I became clearer about how I want (and we need) to live in the twenty-first century.

As a child I learned the first rule of collecting: If you have two of anything, and you find a third, you have a "collection." It was fun. I collected bottle caps, pictures of Farah Fawcett, model rockets, sea glass, coins, stamps, stickers, cards, and the list goes on. As a teenager, I honed the skill of acquisition. I earned a bit of money, learned to shop, and received gifts. My collections grew more sophisticated. Fiestaware was a passion, and the junk stores near my university fed my fever.

There was a brief moment of sanity in my early 20s, when I moved into New York with nothing — just some clothes, a mattress and a stack of books. It was a Bohemian fantasy that was doomed by need and the possibility to score all those great things people left on the streets. I did not learn the beauty of control until I became a designer in my late 20s. And it took me another ten years to begin to apply that control to my own life. But finally, blissfully, I did. There is great freedom in letting go.

The editing process for me started for real with the death of my grandmother and aunt. If I had kept everything that had sentimental value or might have been worth something someday I would have suffocated, so I needed some rules. If it was to be kept, it had to be cared for and used. Paintings were cleaned and framed. I found a restorer for a model boat my dad had made. A mixed bag of chairs was unified by staining and re-caning. The process was expensive, and seemingly endless, but it forced me to commit in some way to the things I would keep.

One of my favorite pieces of "art" came out of this process. It is a series of photographs taken by my grandfather. He was a developer on the Jersey shore and at some point he needed to post "Private Beach" signs. He must have done some research and taken pictures of other signs before he had his own made. I chose four of his 2- by 2-inch photos and had them matted in one frame, arranged horizontally. They hold all the mystery of a contemporary photo essay — distant but intriguing content. I love having preserved a little bit of family history, and framing these allowed me to discard the other two hundred family photos, guilt-free.

The most interesting homes are a reflection of a life well lived. Beauty, quality, history, and value are all good reasons to keep something, but there is nothing better than meaning. Take, for example, my newly restored model boat. There is a big market for model boats these days, and I love to sail. But because they are an old-guard decorating cliché, I would never have gone out and bought one. Nonetheless, I delight in having had this family heirloom restored. Through the process I learned something about model boats, thought about my Dad, and in my highly designed life the model boat is actually a bit of a non-sequitur.

So how do you make choices? 1. Follow your instincts, but don't let sentiment rule. Just because you've had something for a long time, or it came from your family, or is old, or it was a gift, does not make it worth keeping. 2. Keep the real stuff. It's better to have one real antique than a roomful of fakes. 3. Hang on to the things you know something about, and build on that. If you have three pieces of pottery, invest in some books on ceramics and learn about the larger context to develop your interest. 4. Sell a few mediocre items to buy one outstanding piece. Learning to discern is part of the fun, and in the end the goal is to have just a few really good things.

Live a collected life. Home design magazines are great inspiration; they are always featuring things by color, subject matter, material, shape, or concept in their stories. But, don't just coordinate furnishings, arrange them. The objective for me is not to match a mauve sofa with pink drapery, but to focus attention and start a dialogue between the objects. Framing artwork and placing sculpture on pedestals are time-tested ways to focus the eye, or try a built-in display. Find furniture that will accommodate your arrangements. Break up collections and move things frequently so you can see them again in different contexts.

Most likely, the stories in your life are already there. They just need to be brought out and developed. One of the best stories I ever created was an accident. I hung a small Roy Lichtenstein dot-pattern plate on dot-patterned wallpaper, but the arrangement did not really come to life until the day I brought home a speckled orchid and put it on the counter. Art, design, and nature all connected through the dot patterns and it was spectacular.

I turned 40 in the year 2004, and my micro challenge as I headed into my 40s mirrored the challenge to our society as a whole as it goes forward into the twenty-first century: How will we undo the excesses of the complex world we made in the twentieth century? It will certainly mean bucking years of conditioning. I used the occasion to get even more serious about paring down my possessions. The editing process, in turn, defined how I will accumulate things in the future — more carefully than ever before.

My 40th birthday party was fantastic. All of my nearest and dearest gathered, but I forgot to say "no gifts" on the invitation, and people were very generous. I was truly embarrassed by the bounty, but it brought home my truth: What I need in my life is more friends and fewer things. I crave a smaller personal carbon footprint. I'd like one fine truffle risotto rather than the all-you-can-eat buffet, one beautifully executed painting instead of wall-to-wall posters. If we are to live in harmony with the environment, the challenges to our world are certainly bigger than just editing our possessions. But an important component of our new reality will be for each of us to welcome living with less.

❋31❋

Don't dye your hair

After the shock of being ma'am'ed wears off,
this essayist decides to stick with the gray hair
she has earned.

by Elizabeth Peavey

Elizabeth Peavey is the author of *Outta My Way: An Odd Life Lived Loudly* and *Maine & Me, 10 Years of Down East Adventures*, which was awarded the 2006 Maine Literary Award for Best Maine-themed Book. Her essays and articles appear frequently in *Down East* magazine, where she has been a contributing editor since 1997. Her current humor column, "Outta My Yard," can be read online at thebollard.com.

It all started with a simple word, an itty bitty contraction that threw my world into a paroxysm of feminist ageist angst and conflict. The word in question?

Ma'am.

Now, I'm 48. I've been called ma'am plenty since I turned 40, usually by well-meaning baristas or bag boys, who pack no more import behind the address than when they tell me to "Have a good one," which makes me want to swat them and respond "A good what? you English language strangling moron" — which, by the way, is a very ma'amish thing to do, so I don't.

And that's because I'm not a ma'am. I dress like a six-year-old and act like a prepubescent boy. I am downtown and rock 'n' roll. I like to hang upside-down, go fast, be loud, and behave in myriad other unladylike ways that would curl the hairs on most real ma'ams' chins. Really, by all accounts, I could probably pass for much younger than I am. There's just one problem: my hair is gray.

This is not a new development. I got my first gray hair when I was 27, the year after my dad died unexpectedly. I shrieked when I saw it, but quite frankly, I was half-expecting at the time to wake up one morning with a head of white hair. I think I had read somewhere that a deep shock can do that to a person. Or maybe I saw it on a made-for-TV movie. Anyway, the overnight transformation didn't come. The going-gray thing was gradual, one strand at a time, over 20 years.

Early on, my friend Joyce, who likes to boss me around, nagged me to have my hair colored. "Come on. You need to get rid of that mousey brown. You should get some highlights — or why don't you go red?" she'd cajole, and I'd pretend to think this was a good idea long enough to have her finish pouring me a beer or making me supper, then I'd change the subject. After all, I had a look to protect. I was Cute Slob Girl. Slob Girls don't get their hair cut on a regular basis, don't do their nails, don't wear heels, don't iron, don't match, don't mewl over the latest trends. And they definitely don't color their hair — unless it's fuchsia, which I did to my Rod Stewart shag during the '80s, but we don't need to visit that fashion choice again, do we? To color one's hair requires a commitment, a promise to maintain the relationship. I was not up to the task.

But I was lucky. I got away with this Slob Girl look for probably more years than I should've. I got carded well into my 30s. I hung around with friends 10-plus years my junior, perpetuating the myth. I even found and married a man who thinks I'm cuter when I'm dressed like a bag of dirty laundry than when I'm dolled up for a night on the town. Not to mention the fact I've never had a bathroom with decent lighting in it.

And then one day I ran into an acquaintance I'd not seen in some time. I was heading west, and the sun was streaming at me. The friend seemed shocked at the sight of me. During the whole conversation, she stared at my hair and wore a look that said, "Dear God, what happened to Liz Peavey?"

I, of course, just assumed a pigeon had pooed on my head, and the friend was too polite to say so. When I got home, however, and did a full examination, I discovered the cause of her horror: The few gray strands that had been intermittently insinuating themselves over the years had joined forces and formed flanks. Liz Peavey was officially gray.

A decision was called for. Age changes things. Just as there is a fine line between being considered witty and sardonic and just plain bitchy, I could no longer pass myself off as Cute Slob Girl. If I were to keep the gray, I would be making a statement, sending a message to my younger sisters in the trenches: No, to youth worship! Yes, to aging gracefully! Each of my gray hairs represented every wrong turn and turbulence, all my disappointments and good fights. They were a record of my experience, and I was keeping them. Besides, I was too lazy to do anything about it.

And then the ma'am incident occurred.

I was at a bar in town with a group of friends, mostly male, mostly older than I. (No offense to them, but it was not like I was surrounded by hunks.) We arrived en masse, and in fine fettle we crowded up to the rail. The young barmaid waited on the person on either side of me and then every single patron surrounding me, passing me by time and again. Just as I thought I might place an order, her eyes drifted behind me to someone who had just arrived. The gent very courteously pointed out that I had been waiting longer than he. Even then, I was ready to chalk it up, let it go, be OK about it, but then she turned to me with a look that said, "What."

Now here's the thing: I have manned many bars and waited on countless tables in my life. No one does surly public servant better than I did, but this was beyond the pale. This was war.

I will spare you the details of what followed, but picture a shootout between the old sheriff and the young gunslinger that has just ridden into town. They're both holding their own — ptwing! ptwing! — and it looks like it's going to end in a draw, but then a final shot — blam — takes the old timer down. In this case, for me, it was when this barmaid returned with my change, gave me a long lean look directly in the eye and said, "There you go, Ma'am."

I gripped my chest and reeled around the room, knocked over a couple barstools and hit the floor. My campadres circled round as I sputtered these dying words: "She ma'am'ed me, boys. It's over."

OK, so maybe it wasn't that dramatic, but she got to me. When I sat down, I couldn't choke down my beer fast enough. My male friends teased me about starting a cat fight, about having to leave, and I kidded back, but my throat was tight and tears stung my eyes. This wasn't supposed to happen to me. This was supposed to happen to other women — all those real ma'ams — not Action Girl.

And that's when I started thinking about dyeing my hair. My 30th high school reunion was fast approaching. (OK, only a total loser dyes her hair before the first reunion she's ever attended, but I still had time.) I even asked friends for the names of their colorists. Kim offered to go with me. Joyce cheered. And yet, I just never quite made the call. I went to my reunion — I looked fine — and quickly forgot about the whole thing.

When I recounted all this to my friend Deb and her teenage daughter, Cady (who by the way, I have known since birth and who says she can't wait to have her flame-red hair go gray), Cady took it in and asked with the insight only the young seem to have, "Why did you want to color your hair? Was it a self-esteem issue?"

No, I said. It was not because I wanted to appear younger than I am — but because I didn't want to disappear. I thought if I could trick the calendar, play out the clock a little longer . . . I didn't really know where I was going with this.

Cady's gaze was intent, she listened to each word. I was not invisible. I was right there before her. I knew at that moment I had made the right choice.

Besides, as Joyce — who was disappointed by my decision — reminded me, I'd be hard-pressed to find "Mousey Slob-Girl Brown" in a bottle.

32

Color your future

A color expert and strategist encourages
you to take stock in your color of choice
and gain some color confidence.

by Leslie Harrington, PhD

Leslie Harrington is the principal of LH Color and has previously
held various senior management positions in the area of color
strategy and color marketing. She has been quoted and her work
published in *The New York Times*, *The Chicago Tribune*, *Glamour*,
Cosmopolitan, and *US News & World Report*. Leslie is the author
of *Color — A Stroke of Brilliance* and *The Art of Exterior Painting*
and has made numerous TV appearances as a color authority.

As children, we almost all have a favorite color.
It may be evident in the clothes we wore, or the
crayon we most often chose from the box, or even the
color of our favorite stuffed animal. As you continued to
move through life, color may have been one of the few
constants that stayed with you. Perhaps in your 20s you
were able to exercise your color choices in a big way by
buying a certain color car, or painting the walls of your
first apartment.

While these color preferences seemed to be your own, to some degree they most likely were a reaction to the conditioning of your younger years. Beginning in pre-school, or maybe even earlier, we condition children to associate colors to specific things, attributes, and emotions. Yellow is sunshine, clean and happy. Blue is the sky, relaxing and mellow. Perhaps even a gender designation was applied in your family — pink for girls and blue for boys. There were rules that most of us eventually learned: The sun is yellow; a tree is green and brown; the sky is blue.

But now that you are a 40-something, I bet you have developed a new sense of color confidence. (If not, what are you waiting for?) Your colors of choice have evolved over the last 20 years. They are more informed and based on your increasing years of personal experience, experimentations, and your overall self-confidence (translation: you no longer give a damn what others think). You have learned to stand up for your color rights. If you want an orange Range Rover, you buy it. If you desire purple cowboy boots with brown fringe, you buy them. By now, you should be at a point in life where you know what you want and want what you need.

If you have not gained much color confidence over these four decades, it is time to explore this part of your life. If you are still asking family and friends what they think before you commit to a color for a new car, sofa, or dress, you need to consider this area of your life. Are you cladding yourself in black because you heard it makes you look thinner, or perhaps just because it is the simple way out? What worked when you were in your 20s says something different to the world now that you are in your 40s.

Before you get ahead of yourself, don't read this as a license to jump into the color pool without first learning to swim. If you venture in too deep, mixing like mad all the colors of the rainbow, you will risk being tagged as having a midlife crisis! So where is the first place to learn how to swim with colors? Books can be helpful, but they are not my first choice. I believe we all come with an inherit understanding of color and what we need from it. We just have to start slowly and build our confidence. Sure, there might be a few bumps along the way, but for the most part, your days will feel refreshed when you move toward more color.

Color & Personality

Let's get back to our favorite colors. While we all felt very confident about our favorite colors as kids, those alliances may fade or be confused as adults. The associations we have with colors also come with a great deal more depth now that we are older and wiser. Some people say that your favorite color can tell a lot about your personality. While it might sound like cheap astrology, no matter who I bump into they are always interested in what their favorite color says about them. Here's the color chart for 40-somethings as I see it:

Red 40s love life and tend to live life to its fullest. They search for richness and adventure. Never tell a red friend a secret, as they are less likely to keep it than any other color lover. Being a red person, you will probably find yourself restless in your 40s, and thus looking to get out of dodge.

Orange 40s are known for their warm, friendly demeanor. They have passion for their family and their home. They make great friends and will be there to help pick up the pieces should you fall apart at this time of your life.

Yellow 40s are known for their intellect. Thinkers and tinkers, yellow lovers are still likely on a path of learning and probably never stopped. Yellow 40-year-olds are probably considering going back to school or changing careers.

Green 40s are known for their concentration and collaboration. Looking for someone to help with a new venture? Select a green person. Being green also means that you are to some extent materialistic. You love the finer things in life and feel that at this point in your life, you surely deserve them. It is possible that you are spending more money than you ever have in your life.

Blue 40s have long been known as tried and true, not to mention trustworthy. Many of us see ourselves with these characteristics. Interestingly, blue is the most preferred color in the world, bar none. As a blue person, you should also be aware that you are identified as having a strong sex drive (like you didn't already know), and especially at this time in your life it might feel like an extra sense of renewed energy.

Purple 40s is a fence-sitting color. Purple lovers exhibit characteristics of both blues and reds. Thus you are a passionate person looking for adventure, all stimulated by your strong sex drive. Watch out world as the purples really come unleashed as they head into their 40s.

White 40s remain the epitome of purity and innocence. For those of us who do not choose white as our most preferred or dominant color, we still know how to leverage it to communicate to others when we wish to be perceived in an innocent light. If you truly prefer white as you move into your 40s, chances are you are ready to settle down to a less pressured life.

Black 40s prefer not to commit themselves, but rather keep an open mind to decide on an issue later. At some level this might seem conservative, but it's more about living with things for a bit before changing. You tend to have strong confidence in everything but your ability to live with color.

If you are confident in your colors of choice, go forth and allow those colors to mature with you. If you remain a 40-year-old with a confused color palate, take it slowly, notice the colors around you, but make your own choices with intention.

33

Grow a garden

Author of "The Cranky Gardner" column,
Deborah Needleman proposes that you measure
your life with nature as a yardstick.

by Deborah Needleman

Deborah Needleman is the founding editor in chief of *domino* magazine. In its first year, *domino* was honored with every major media award for best new magazine and Needleman was named "One to Watch" by *Women's Wear Daily*. Her writing on gardens and design has appeared in *Slate*, where she penned "The Cranky Gardener" column, *House & Garden*, and *The New York Times*.

As a rule, young people don't think much about gardening. It is not edgy or cool, it rarely leads to sex, and celebrities don't ever get their picture taken doing it. It is, however, the only thing I have ever done precociously. Not that I did it particularly well, it's just that I started early — in my second decade rather than my fourth or fifth.

I did it passionately, rushing into the yard every morning to see what was new, and never wanting to stop for dinner or because it was getting dark. Gardening has sustained me over the years, and the only way I can envision myself as an old woman is in the garden. It is a pursuit that you actually improve at, the older you get. And the same goes for the garden: The older it gets, the lovelier it becomes.

Gardening's chief recommendations, however, diverge pretty sharply from the way it is typically celebrated — as a pleasant and useful hobby with therapeutic effects. Gardening is kind of absurd, and this is a great part of its charm. It is not really practical, and that includes growing your own vegetables.

Consider that you must locate and lay out the plot; hire a contractor to dig the area and put in a fence; amend the soil; buy seeds, plants, fertilizers, stakes, etc. This, so you can spend untold hours over the next five months nurturing your harvest to fruition. Come the day you pluck that juicy heirloom tomato, it ends up costing more than dinner at a fancy restaurant.

"Ahh, but gardening is relaxing," people say. This I have never understood. Gardening is hours of tedious and repetitive work crouched over in the hot sun, doing battle with weeds bent on world domination and pests for whom your blossoms constitute a four-star meal, and coping with premature deaths and other natural calamities. All the while, your children plead for lunch or simply for their neglect to end. I enjoy spending my time this way immensely. I just find it stressful.

Preserving a fragile ecosystem makes sense, but making a garden is a folly. It's wonderful precisely because we choose to do it — to wrestle and engage with nature — when we really don't have to. Gardening's utter needlessness and its commitment only to beauty is what makes it so poignantly human.

Of course, gardening can yield some fine results — bouquets for the table, veggies for cooking, and areas of cultivated distinction surrounding the home. But those are really the extras. Gardening is not about the ends, it's about the means, and about what the means all mean.

Henry James discerningly singled out the words "summer afternoon" as the most beautiful in the English language. I, however, relish nearly the entire vocabulary of the garden: "gathering flowers," "laying in the grass," "a lane of old trees," "the evening's fragrance," "under the oak tree," "mama's in the garden." These phrases got to me before I ever got my hands dirty. The ideas, associations, and memories of gardening — both my own and other peoples, are what drove my passion to begin DOING it.

As a gardener, you get free membership in a club of fantastically eccentric people — literary geniuses, plant-mad obsessives, bohemian dilettantes, visionary architects and landscape designers, inbred royals, and officious garden club ladies. These people, whether they know of me or not, and mostly they do not, make my world bigger and richer.

It thrills me to have a connection to a paunchy, old galanthophile (snowdrop flower enthusiast), who fixates on the minutiae of the markings on the half-inch flower of his 4-inch plant. Ditto, all the wildly stylish, tough, aristocratic English gardening ladies, from Vita Sackville West to the dowager Duchess of Devonshire. Ditto, Edith Wharton and her bold 1904 carriage tour of Italian Renaissance gardens, which I used as my itinerary nearly a hundred years later, with her fantastic descriptions as my guide and companion. Yes, these are my peeps.

I don't know why, but I have always wanted fabulous old lady friends, and gardening gave me a path to them. My first and dearest, Risi, shares her spreading daffodils with me, offers us fresh eggs, and always has cookies for the children, even if she can't remember my name so well now. Risi is 90, but she still manages to have a lovely table centerpiece and twinned mantel arrangements year round, picked from the garden — even if they're just holly or ivy. The image of her graciousness at a luncheon until the precise moment when she decides it's over for her and she bolts for her garden, is locked in my heart.

Gardening is sweaty, tactical labor, so sweet because it is totally engrossing work that is completely outside daily routines. Gardening yields focus, absorption, and awe. It is wondrous and up-close and pays no attention to you. Your perennial borders don't care that you've gained ten pounds or that you had a bad day at the office.

Nature neither needs nor notices you, but tending a plot gives you a tiny way into its big, careless drama. As soon as you plant a bulb in the fall and it pushes up in the spring, you've gained a little toehold. Our lives no longer really require us to participate in the cycle of the natural world, but gardening allows you to force yourself (very gently) back into it. The more I insert myself, the more I depend on it.

I love the connection to the seasons so badly that it fills me with melancholy and nostalgia before they have even passed. I conscientiously take in the moments prior to spring's main events: the bright color rising in the branches of the willow before it leafs out, the delicate chartreuse flowers dropping from the bare branches of the sugar maple, and the gingko's perfect-pleated leaves opening like translucent fans. As a defense, I try to parse the seasons. If I can keep slicing spring into smaller and smaller parts by witnessing its every attribute, will it, like Zeno's paradox, never end?

The panic I feel at time's flight is met in equal measure by the precious solace of seeing beauty that I know won't last. My life is marked, land-marked really, by the appearance and location and scent of plants. I can name the weeks by their smell, as the winter gives way to the first honeysuckle, then viburnum, then lilac...to the days when the dogrose wafts up from the marsh.

I have no idea how long I've been married to my husband or what year we met, but I remember how things felt between us when all these plants bloomed for the first time, and the second time, and every year thereafter. I don't really know what goes through the minds of my children when they eat their way through the vegetable garden in their bare feet or pick flowers for a bouquet for their mother, but I know what goes through mine.

34

How to survive your 40s

A witty and frank *coming-of-age* essay about facing daily life as a contemporary forty-something woman.

by Pamela Druckerman

Pamela Druckerman is the author of four books including *Bringing Up Bébé: One American Mother Discovers the Wisdom of French Parenting*, which has been translated into 27 languages. She's also a contributing opinion writer at *The New York Times*.

I f you want to know how old you look, just walk into a French cafe. It's like a public referendum on your face.

When I moved to Paris in my early 30s, waiters called me "mademoiselle." It was "Bonjour, mademoiselle" when I walked into a cafe and "Voilà, mademoiselle" as they set down a coffee.

Around the time I turned 40, however, there was a collective switch, and waiters started calling me "madame." These "madames" were tentative at first, but soon they were coming at me like a hailstorm. Now it's "Bonjour, madame" when I walk in, "Merci, madame" when I pay my bill and "Au revoir, madame" as I leave. Sometimes several waiters shout this at once.

On one hand, I'm intrigued by this transition. Do these waiters gather after work for Sancerre and a slide show to decide which female customers to downgrade? (Irritatingly, men are "monsieur" forever.)

The worst part is that they're trying to be polite. They believe I'm old enough that the title can't possibly wound.

I realize that something has permanently shifted when I walk past a woman begging for money.

"Bonjour, mademoiselle," she calls out to the young woman in a miniskirt a few steps ahead of me.

"Bonjour, madame," she says when I pass.

This has all happened too quickly for me to digest. I still have most of the clothes that I wore as a mademoiselle. There are mademoiselle-era cans of food in my pantry.

But the world keeps telling me that I've entered a new stage. While studying my face in a well-lit elevator, my daughter describes it bluntly: "Mommy, you're not old, but you're definitely not young."

What exactly is this not-young age? I hear people in their 20s describe the 40s as a far-off decade of too-late, when they'll regret things that they haven't done.

But for older people I meet, the 40s are the decade that they would most like to travel back to. "How could I possibly have thought of myself as old at 40?" asks Stanley Brandes, an anthropologist who wrote a book in 1985 about turning 40. "I sort of look back and think: God, how lucky I was. I see it as the beginning of life, not the beginning of the end."

Forty isn't even technically middle age anymore. Someone who's now 40 has a 50 percent chance of living to 95, says the economist Andrew Scott, a co-author of *The 100-Year Life.*

But the number 40 still has symbolic resonance. Jesus fasted for 40 days. Muhammad was 40 when the archangel Gabriel appeared to him. The Israelites wandered the desert for 40 years. Mr. Brandes writes that in some languages, 40 means "a lot."

And age 40 still feels pivotal. "The 40s are when you become who you are," a British author in his 70s tells me, adding ominously, "And if you don't know by your 40s, you never will."

I'm starting to see that as a madame, even a newly minted one, I am subject to new rules. When I try to act adorably naïve now, people aren't charmed — they're baffled. Cluelessness no longer goes with my face. I'm expected to wait in the correct line at airports and show up on time for my appointments.

And yet brain research shows that in the 40s, some of these tasks are harder: On average we're more easily distracted than younger people, we digest information more slowly and we're worse at remembering specific facts. (The ability to remember names peaks in the early 20s.) You know you're in your 40s when you've spent 48 hours trying to think of a word, and that word was "hemorrhoids."

But there are upsides, too. What we lack in processing power we make up for in maturity, insight and experience. We're better than younger people at grasping the essence of situations, controlling our emotions and resolving conflicts. We're more skilled at managing money and explaining why things happen. We're more considerate than younger people. And, crucially for our happiness, we're less neurotic.

Indeed, modern neuroscience and psychology confirm what Aristotle said more than 2,000 years ago when he described men in their "primes" as having "neither that excess of confidence which amounts to rashness, nor too much timidity, but the right amount of each. They neither trust everybody nor distrust everybody, but judge people correctly."

I agree. We've actually managed to learn and grow a bit. We see the hidden costs of things. Our parents have stopped trying to change us. We can tell when something is ridiculous. And other minds are finally less opaque. The seminal journey of the 40s is from "everyone hates me" to "they don't really care."

Even so, the decade is confusing. We can finally decode interpersonal dynamics, but we can't remember a two-digit number. We're at or approaching our lifetime peak in earnings, but Botox now seems like a reasonable idea. We're reaching the height of our careers, but we can now see how they will probably end.

And this new age is strangely lacking in milestones. Childhood and adolescence are nothing but milestones: You grow taller, advance to new grades, and get your period, your driver's license and your diploma. Then in your 20s and 30s you romance potential partners, find jobs and learn to support yourself. There may be promotions, babies and weddings. The pings of adrenaline from all these carry you forward and reassure you that you're building an adult life.

In the 40s, we might still acquire degrees, jobs, homes and spouses, but these elicit less wonder now. The mentors and parents who used to rejoice in our achievements are preoccupied with their own declines. If we have kids, we're supposed to marvel at their milestones. A journalist I know lamented that he'd never again be a prodigy at anything. (Someone younger than both of us had just been nominated to the United States Supreme Court.)

"Even five years ago, people I met would be like, 'Wow, you're the boss?'" the 44-year-old head of a TV production company tells me. Now they're matter-of-fact about his title. "I've aged out of wunderkind," he says.

What have we aged into? We're still capable of action, change and 10K races. But there's a new immediacy to the 40s — and an awareness of death — that didn't exist before. Our possibilities feel more finite. All choices now plainly exclude others. It's pointless to keep pretending to be what we're not. At 40, we're no longer preparing for an imagined future life. Our real lives are, indisputably, happening right now. We've arrived at what Immanuel Kant called the "Ding an sich" — the thing itself.

Indeed, the strangest part of the 40s is that we're now the ones attending parent-teacher conferences and cooking the turkey on Thanksgiving. These days, when I think, "Someone should really do something about that," I realize with alarm that that "someone" is me.

It's not an easy transition. I'd always been reassured by the idea that there are grown-ups in the world out there curing cancer and issuing subpoenas. Grown-ups fly airplanes, get aerosol into bottles and make sure that television signals are magically transmitted. They know whether a novel is worth reading and which news belongs on the front page. In an emergency, I've always trusted that grown-ups — mysterious, capable and wise — would appear to rescue me.

I'm not thrilled about looking older. But what unsettles me most about the 40s is the implication that I'm now a grown-up myself. I fear I've been promoted beyond my competence. What is a grown-up anyway? Do they really exist? If so, what exactly do they know? Will my mind ever catch up with my face?

Section Six

KEEP IT IN BALANCE

35

What to know about turning 40

This best-selling author asks her friends and mentors to share their wisdom on turning 40.

by Samantha Ettus

Samantha Ettus is a best-selling author, media personality, entrepreneur and speaker, passionate about helping working moms to design a successful and happy lifestyle. Samantha hosts a weekly radio show and is a contributor to *Forbes*. Connect with her at sam@ workingmomslifestyle.com or @samanthaettus.

At every age, I have been a bit proud of the year under my belt. But this one is different. My 40th birthday arrives this week and I have become a wreck. I want a party. I don't want a party. I am sad. I am hysterical. I have everything I have always wanted. I just want to crawl under the covers.

I am often accused of being that woman — the one that appears to have it all together. Whose Facebook page looks like a highlight reel, whose kids look at the camera in synch for the holiday photo, but at the end of the day, we are all busy fighting our own struggles and assuming others' don't exist. And I find that working moms, especially, worry in silos. We don't think we have time to compare notes so we struggle alone, feeling misunderstood and overwhelmed.

So instead of bottling my 40-phobia away, I decided to contact some friends and mentors (who I have always thought of as having it all!) and seeing how 40 looked from their pedestals. Given what I do, they are a group of women with careers in the media. I am grateful for their refreshingly candid reflections and thrilled to share them with you:

Suzy Welch, 52, author of *10-10-10*

"At 39, I was a senior editor at *Harvard Business Review*, working 40-plus hours a week and loving it very much indeed, but also holding down the fort at home with four kids aged ten, nine, seven, and five. My life in that period was so frantic, and the logistics were so complicated, that I used a color-coded calendar to make it through the days without missing a meeting or leaving a kid at soccer practice. As I saw 40 looming, my thoughts were not very profound, I'm afraid to say, as daily survival, as a professional and as a mother, was my main objective. Basically, I wouldn't go back there again if you paid me a billion dollars.

"In my 40s, I discovered that huge debacles in life, say,

like being fired in a highly public brouhaha, do not actually kill you. It is OK to fall down. It is OK to make mistakes. It is OK to take risks. You will live another day and you will be fine. Your 40s are when you start seeing glimmers of what will become your wisdom. In your 30s, you're having a lot of varied experiences. You're scrambling. You're putting pieces in place. In your 40s, those pieces start to coalesce into knowledge about who you are and how life works."

Natalie Tysdal, 41, TV Anchor

"Forty hit me hard. I had my third and final baby the year before after two miscarriages and I think it was the first birthday where I didn't feel invincible. A few gray hairs, a few wrinkles, and a few more pounds. I felt like I was slowing down. I didn't like that feeling so I did something about it.

"I climbed my first 14er, a mountain that I was not going to let define my age. I'm not a climber or even an expert athlete. It was the hardest thing outside of childbirth I have ever done. The conditions for climbing were extreme and I wanted to quit a hundred times. I kept telling myself, just one more stretch up the mountain, just one more rock. And when we reached the top I cried like a baby. I couldn't believe I made it.

"Being over 40 makes me feel 'seasoned.' I may hide a few wrinkles and grey hair but I'll never hide my age. Never!"

Lee Woodruff, 52, Author of *In an Instant*

"I absolutely loved turning 40 — it didn't feel awful to me — it felt like coming into my own. I was in great health, we were moving to England and my twins had just been born. For the first (and probably only) time in my life we threw a massive going away/twins born/turning 40 party in our backyard. I cooked most of the food and strung tea lights in the trees. I remember thinking that I felt as if 40 meant I was finally wise enough to give advice and be taken seriously but still young enough that the world offered the upward trajectory of possibility."

Tory Johnson, 41, Founder, Spark and Hustle
"In the year leading up to it, I wanted a big party, but as the month approached, I decided to have a very low key celebration with my immediate family despite my husband's protest. He thought I deserved a big bash. I refused. So he bought me an over-the-top diamond bangle from Tiffany's (my only jewelry from there!) to mark the occasion. I wear it every day as a symbol of moving into a new decade.

"Perhaps that's a benefit of 40 — better jewelry, which is ironic, since jewelry and other material things mean so much less to me as I get older. I loved my 30s and wasn't sure how I'd feel turning 40, but I'm more confident and comfortable at 41. My kids, 15-year-old twins who were born when I was 26, still think I'm a 'young mom,' which sounds cool to me."

Liz Lange, 43, Designer
"Forty definitely felt like a big milestone and I was annoyed at myself for not having felt younger in my 30s as it's only once you are about to turn 40 that you realize how young your 30s really are. I love being in my 40s and for me it is a new chapter,

I am divorced and starting new businesses. My 30s were all about founding and building Liz Lange Maternity and having my children. My 40s are all about the next phase."

Gretchen Rubin, 46, Author, *The Happiness Project*
"It felt like a big milestone and a bit intimidating. I remember reading somewhere that 'the 40s are the old age of youth, and the youth of old age,' and that seems true to me. Though I expected that turning 40 would make me feel more like a real "grown-up" at last, in fact, I didn't feel anymore adult. I still don't. My father told me he was almost 60 before he felt like a true grown-up.

"It was a very busy time, so I didn't do anything special. My husband knew that I admired a particular watch, so he bought it for me for no reason, but because it was near my birthday, we decided after the fact to treat it as a 40th-birthday gift. I was more touched that he'd bought it for no reason than I would have been if he'd picked it out for my birthday! I still wear it every day, so it was a perfect milestone gift.

"As I've gotten older, and since I've spent so much time thinking about happiness, I've done a much better job about shaping my life to reflect my own nature, interests, and values. I try to 'Be Gretchen' and not worry about what I think ought to be true or what other people expect or value."

Naomi Wolf, 49, Founder of DailyCloudt.com

"I was pretty happy and definitely in the thick of it — small children, busy career, helping to run a family. I never felt that worried about turning 40 because my mother is vibrant, radiant, and youthful in her outlook, so age always seemed like a number.

"Still, it freaked me out — I do recall after the big birthday I was surprised that I didn't feel at all like a grown-up, but just the same. I also felt some relief that I had worked so hard in my 20s and 30s because I definitely did not feel like I had gotten nothing done and time was passing. I did also feel a wish to reevaluate and make sure that everything in my life was there for a good reason. Time didn't seem endless anymore.

"I definitely feel more in charge of my life now; I have a better understanding I think of how the world works. I enjoy other people in this decade more, they are more ready to be on a quest and less status-oriented and less striving — those were the 30s, in NY and DC anyway, socially, and I found that tiresome.

"People in their 40s have a greater sense of self, for better or worse. Superficial people are more clear that that is what they are and deep people are easier to spot too. I love every stage of being a mom but it is so great to have older kids with wonderful ideas to discuss."

36

Power up your activism

Ten prioritized points from the former president
of the Sierra Club to help you to engage
in the natural world.

by Lisa Renstrom

Lisa Renstrom served as the 51st president of the Sierra Club from
2005-2007. She received her Bachelors of Science degree with a
focus in finance from the business school at the University of
Nebraska and attended Harvard Business School's Owner President
Management Program. When Lisa stepped down from her term at
the Sierra Club, she biked from the California-Oregon Border to
San Francisco.

When I turned 40, I felt that I had walked over
the threshold to adulthood. You're busy in
your 20s figuring out life, and in your 30s, you spend a
lot of effort performing and "norming," i.e. learning to
conform to the "normal" world. The wonderful thing
about turning 40 is that you can use the experience
and wisdom and new-found adulthood to influence the
world around you. I did so by becoming involved in the
environmental movement, or what is now becoming the
climate movement.

So this is my list, in priority order, of what to do when you turn 40 to take advantage of all that natural life offers:

1. Figure out what your carbon footprint is, find the efficiencies you are missing, cut your costs and carbon, then reduce it by 5 percent annually until you turn 90. Your carbon footprint is just that — how much carbon dioxide or CO_2 you emit by virtue of living on this planet (just google "carbon footprint" and you will turn up dozens of sites that will walk you through what it means and how to do this). It is educational, interesting, and will change the way you think about most everything you do.

2. Become engaged in this burgeoning climate movement. We have until 2015 to change the trajectory of greenhouse gas emissions. Talk to friends and neighbors, business colleagues, and everyone you know about how we will move America to a post-carbon culture and economy.

3. If you haven't communed with nature since you were 10, plant something and nurture it. Close your eyes and listen to the birds. Find a river that is fit to swim in and dive in. Walk in the rain, in a forest, or through a meadow. Do something that reminds you that you are part of this planet and its life-giving forces. If expeditious, you can seek experiences like this in your local park, or clean up and enjoy a bit of the empty lot across the street.

4. Grow food. Whether in your backyard or in a window box. Plant something that you can watch as it grows. Harvest and eat it with great appreciation for the taste and sustenance it gives you. According to a study in the *Journal of Neuroscience*, exposure to soil may be a way to lift mood as well as boost the immune system!

5. Buy a bird feeder or a birdbath and become mesmerized by these fantastic creatures that migrate and flitter all around us. Birds weigh merely ounces, yet have distinct personalities and can transport themselves across whole continents.

6. Forty is a great time to become part of the civic society that holds our democracy together. Join a local organization that works to make your community a better place for you and yours. Join a national organization that promotes social justice, human rights, and the environment. Go to a city council meeting or to the wellness committee at a local grade school (to ensure that foods on school menus contribute to health and wellness, rather than obesity and sickness). If they don't have one, form one.

Those are my recommendations as an environmentalist — must-do's from the tree-hugger side of me. However, I am not a one-note person any more than you are, so

I'll share five more that have served me well.

7. Know that you look really good for 40! If you look back at pictures of yourself when you were 25, 30, or 35, you'll remember that at that time, you found flaws in your appearance. But, now when you go back through old photos, you probably realize how marvelous you actually were. So as you turn 40, realize that when you look from the vantage point of age 50, you will again realize that you looked marvelous, if only you had known it. So save time and enjoy it now.

8. If you are turning 40, you probably remember Crosby, Stills, Nash, and Young. Take some of their advice, **"Love the one you're with."** This is the moment to go deep again. Do nice things for those you love. Think of what your partner loves to do and do it with him or her. Figure out what is most important to each of you and deliberately let your partner have his or her way. Redirect energy toward making your relationship sparkle.

9. If you've had children, focus your love on them. Don't have more.

10. If you have children, know any, or love any, read *Last Child in the Woods: Nature Deficit Disorder* by Richard Louv. Nature has so much to teach each of us, and if we grow up uncomfortable with dirt and worms or wind and rain, it is we who suffer. Children gain confidence and a greater sense of self if they can connect their lives to the world around them, to people outside their immediate family, to animals, trees and plants, to mountains and rivers.

11. If for any reason you are not fully computer-literate, make it a priority to reach a new comfort level with the technology. The Internet is the new communal civic space. You have to get connected — because we are all in this together.

37

Have a bun and a pizza in the oven

This entrepreneurial baker offers her recipe for having a child, a business, and the best time of her life.

by Amy Scherber

Amy Scherber is the owner of Amy's Bread, the nationally recognized bakery that specializes in hand-made, traditional breads and sweets. After attending the New York Restaurant School, Scherber worked at Bouley and trained in France. She has two production kitchens and 3 retail cafes in New York City, and is the author of *Amy's Bread, Revised and Updated* (Houghton Mifflin Harcourt).

If you're considering starting a family — no matter what your job — don't waste a moment. At this point in your life you are more than ready and so appreciative for the prospect of a baby's arrival. All your experiences provide depth and stability that you can share with this little person. Having a child after age 40 may not be easy, and you'll undoubtedly be a bit more exhausted than those 30-something parents, but it's fantastic. This is my personal journey.

When you start your own business, there is no right time to have a child. Launching a small company is all consuming. It saps your energy and creativity and it takes all your time. My business is a bread bakery, which seems to complicate matters even more. Bakers work all night baking and sleep a few hours during the day. Having a social life is out of the question. The prospect of meeting someone and building a relationship is poor.

I opened my bakery at the age of 32. During the first two years I always worked the overnight shift, but gradually I was able to start leaving by midnight or 1 A.M. For about 5 years, my only night off was Saturday. During that time I went from being engaged and married to being divorced and single. By age 37, I really needed to get out and have some fun. My chances of starting a family were practically non-existent.

I finally began dating someone and started allowing myself to take Wednesday nights as "date night." It was a beginning. By the time I hit 40, I continued to enjoy my Wednesday nights out. But, I was still single and only dreaming of having a child. My doctor had cautioned me to get cracking because time was not on my side.

At last, all those Wednesday dates blossomed into a proposal and marriage. Two years later, after two miscarriages and a lot of effort getting pregnant, I finally had a smooth full-term pregnancy and I gave birth to a beautiful son at age 44.

I have cut my hours to 40 per week and take almost all of my weekends off to enjoy time with my husband and our son. There are advantages to motherhood as a business owner. Once your company is stable, you can set your own schedule and have more flexibility juggling work and childcare. My husband and I take turns dropping our son off and picking him up from day care and babysitting. We both work daytime hours so we can spend our evenings playing at home.

When I come home from my day, my son always greets me at the door to see if I'm carrying bread, then grabs it out of the bag and takes a big bite out of the loaf. He loves bread and adores our trips to the bakery. From the beginning, I couldn't wait for the day he was able to come visit the place and squish little pieces of dough in his hands.

One Saturday when he was just beginning to talk, we stopped at the bakery. He loved to be held next to the industrial-sized mixer to watch the big batch of bread dough turn in the bowl. On this particular day I lifted him up to watch it. He looked inside and said plainly, "dough." It was one of his first words, without prompting. I knew it was almost time for our first baking lesson!

Baking bread with a child is a natural. The feel of the dough, the fun of pushing and pulling it, and the messiness of the work are exhilarating for kids — and adults. Getting tiny hands in dough is satisfying on so many levels. It stimulates all the senses. The sound of making bread is a happy, rhythmic slapping and folding. Everyone loves its floury, yeasty smell. And the look of dough is intriguing. Once it's fully kneaded, it forms a soft, expanding puddle on the countertop, unlike almost anything else.

You don't have to be a pro to make good bread at home. Just try a simple yeasted dough. Baking bread is more interactive than making cookies or preparing a meal because you and your child can both get your hands in the dough at once. Baking in tandem is more about the process than the final product. The pleasure comes from doing it together and sharing the work. You both use some muscle to knead the dough and have fun anticipating the final results.

Pizza — really an Italian quick bread — provides immediate gratification. You can enjoy the fun of mixing and kneading, and since the rising time is much shorter than conventional bread, you get to sample your work a lot sooner. It can even satisfy the attention span of a 2½-year-old. Plus, you can customize the toppings on different portions to suit the taste buds of a child and a 40-something palate.

When we're ready to bake, my 3-year-old old son chooses an apron for both of us. I usually get the funny green one my grandma made. He gets out the scale, the mixing bowl, and the measuring spoons, and climbs up on his little wooden chair so he can reach the counter. I preheat the oven and place a baking stone inside to help the pizza bake faster and get a crispier crust.

We mix the dough in the bowl then move it to the lightly floured counter to knead together. We both push and pull until it becomes elastic and supple. Once the dough's kneaded and has had a little time to rise, we both pat and stretch it into a circle and place it on a cornmeal-covered wooden "peel" (paddle). We top the dough with a mild, chunky tomato sauce and handfuls of grated mozzarella, and slide it onto our stone in the oven. In 10 minutes it's out and we can taste our home-made pizza.

If your child is age appropriate for delayed gratification, choose a basic white or whole-wheat bread recipe. After the dough rises, shape it into a log and bake it in a loaf pan. Forty-five minutes later the kitchen's filled with an irresistible smell and the loaf's done. Give it 20 minutes to cool, then dig in. Nothing will tempt a kid into a good lunch or snack like a sandwich on her own handmade bread. If you don't have a child, borrow one. Make bread or pizza with a niece or nephew, a neighbor, or a friend's child. At every age, baking is its own reward.

38

Connect with your landscape

This decade of your life, when you've achieved some personal and professional success, is a great time to give some attention to the world. A professor of geology, he urges you to become aware of your environmental impact on the earth.

by Douglas M. Thompson

Douglas M. Thompson is a professor of geology and chair of the department of Physics, Astronomy and Geophysics at Connecticut College. A specialist in fluvial geomorphology, his research focuses on the physics of flowing water and its influence on shaping natural rivers and streams through erosion and deposition of sediment. He has been in his current position for ten years and will serve as the associate director of the Goodwin-Niering Center for Conservation Biology and Environmental Studies.

I usually get interesting looks at parties when I tell people, "I am a fluvial geomorphologist." I quickly follow up with, "I study rivers." Perhaps it would be more accurate to say I study landscapes, natural ones mostly. But as you can imagine it is impossible to ignore the human impact on the landscape we inhabit.

At age 40, I have yet to see a river that has not been impacted by humans. Rivers, like most other aspects of the environment, have been hit hard by centuries of manipulation. For this reason and because of my concerns over my 6-year-old daughter's future, I have become increasingly devoted to living an earth-friendly lifestyle that's wary of human impact.

In practice, this means that I work to educate myself continually on ways to live a less wasteful and environmentally-damaging life. I race for Anthem Blue Cross and Blue Shield Cycling Team, an elite amateur team. I find that bicycle racing gives me a much-needed distraction, an athletic outlet, and a source of energy that reinvigorates me. Plus, a bike offers a low impact way to travel.

I don't want to come across as an environmental fanatic determined to preach from his ivory tower. In truth, I decided to become a scientist because I love rivers and wanted to understand how they operate, not because I was trying to save the earth. I like trying to make order out of chaos, and rivers with their turbulent flows, complex histories, and tremendous power to change the landscape offer the perfect challenge.

Change is natural, despite claims to the contrary. This statement is as true for people as it is for landscapes. We will never stop landscape change, but if we make some changes in our personal behavior, we might limit the negative environmental alterations that are so obvious today. After two decades of research, it has become clear to me that science alone can't do the job: The world needs action if we are to save what we value. This decade of your life, when you've achieved some personal and professional success, is a great time to start.

As our society has become increasingly technologically advanced, we have become disconnected from the landscape that we inhabit. It's not that we are less reliant than before on the natural landscape, but that too many of us are just largely ignorant of our role in the ecosystem. I recently judged finalists at the Connecticut State Science Fair, and the types of projects show that our youngest generations are very concerned about the earth. As adults, we have a responsibility to take their legacy seriously. It is, quite simply, a cop-out to be cynical about the fate of the earth and ignore the importance of the common good.

We expect to find exotic fruits in the supermarket year round but have little appreciation for the resources needed to produce that food. We move to the shoreline for its beauty, but destroy the beaches in an effort to protect our homes from the water. Some of us complain about gasoline prices, but then pay more per gallon for bottled water than for gas. And we ignore the oil needlessly used for manufacturing the plastic, transporting the product, and disposing of the bottles.

Now's a great time to become aware of your own environmental impact. Being a good citizen means watching what you waste. Educate yourself about the traces you leave on the earth and start to soften them. I get great pleasure out of fixing objects that are broken, finding new uses for old things, and making due without the latest, greatest gadget. (Is it only the environmentalist in me or also the cheapskate?) I recycle all I can and, consequently, my garbage can is rarely full. I commute to work by bike every chance I get, even during the winter. The sight of my pickup truck sitting unused in the garage at home is inspirational.

Of course, living an environmentally friendly lifestyle is not always straightforward. When I go to the supermarket, I still don't know how to answer the question, "Do you want paper or plastic?" Do we value saving trees or oil? I tend to dodge that question by carrying reusable canvas shopping bags. And, I am unsure of my decision to forego the purchase of a brand new super-efficient car in favor of getting as much use as possible out of my old pickup. As a scientist, I know I am sometimes paralyzed by my tendency to overanalyze in hopes of finding the perfect solution. Ultimately, I realize that not every action can be validated. The most important step is to make environmental concerns part of our everyday decision-making process.

One hundred years from now it is doubtful that anyone will still be reading my papers or indulging my theories on rivers. However, I do hope that my daughter's generation will appreciate the small sacrifices eco-savvy adults make today to ensure the continued existence of a planet that makes us proud. We can all sleep better at night knowing that in doing more good than harm, we can be part of the solution, not the problem. ⇐

39

Seek the spirit — and find it

Deciding to become a mother at 40 changed everything for this Unitarian Universalist chaplain.

by Pamela Barz

Pamela Barz, Unitarian Universalist chaplain at Wellesley College, has served as a parish minister in churches in Maine and Massachusetts. A graduate of Wellesley herself, she also earned a Masters of Divinity at the Harvard Divinity School and currently lives in New Hampshire with her husband and twin sons.

"*The wind of God is always blowing. You just need to hoist your sails,*" an old saying has it. It was when I turned 40 that I finally raised my sails, and the wind hasn't stopped blowing yet.

My 40th birthday wasn't something I looked forward to. I was divorced, childless, and very much wanting a son or daughter before it was too late. But inspired by a friend who'd thrown a party to recognize her own 40-year milestone, I brought a wonderful group of girlfriends together, and we had a beautiful celebration. I was surrounded by love and support. It was one of my favorite birthdays ever.

Soon after, I went on a retreat with a group of other female clergy. We met twice a year and usually reflected on our ministries. But this time we were all at turning points in our personal lives. Retirement, marriage, and children were the questions in our hearts, and we shared these concerns with one another. I don't remember the spark, but I came away deciding to have a child on my own.

The idea had crossed my mind before, but it had always overwhelmed me and I'd put it aside. Now, talking with my colleagues, I realized that this was what God was calling me to do. My deep yearning was not a purposeless desire or a cosmic joke. And I wouldn't be doing this all alone because so many friends were offering help — providing a place to live, acting as a birth coach, babysitting. "I've been waiting for you to realize you could do this!" one of my friends said later.

And so I began the process. I found a supportive doctor who put me in touch with another patient, a mother in my area who had had a child on her own. This woman had found a church that embraced her as a single mother. She told me stories about her life with her daughter, including one encounter with a shopkeeper who'd asked the little girl about her daddy. When she said she had no daddy — that the doctor had helped her mommy become pregnant — the shopkeeper volunteered that she had a niece who also had had a child on her own. This mother's story gave me courage.

I began to tell people about my plans. Two of my friends were willing to be trained to give me the daily hormone shots I would need for four weeks before the in vitro fertilization (IVF) treatments. Key church leaders were also supportive. I would finish my work at the church I was serving, take time off to have the baby, live with friends while I did that, and then find a part-time ministry.

Everything was falling into place, with even the perfect part-time job at Wellesley College becoming available. It wasn't the life I'd envisioned for myself, but it now felt like the right life. Those winds were blowing.

And they kept blowing in ways I'd never have imagined. I had assumed I wouldn't marry again. But I had friends who were meeting people through the Internet, so I decided to give it a try, too. For the first time ever, I had fun dating. I wasn't looking for someone to marry and raise a child with, and that let me relax. I met some pleasant men, saw some interesting movies and plays, and enjoyed myself. But my focus was on a trial IVF cycle going on that summer and preparing myself for the real one to follow.

Then, just before my 41st birthday, I met someone new. I began to realize he was serious about our relationship. When I was with him, I felt I'd come home at last. Now the conversation with my friends was how and when to tell him that I was getting ready to have a child on my own. Some thought I shouldn't tell him at all, because it would push him away. Others thought I owed him the truth. Finally the decision was made for me, when he asked me one night what had been troubling me. I told him the whole story and when I was finished he said, "That's great! You'll be a wonderful mother!" His question was, "How can I be involved?"

So here I am, a few years later, where I never expected to find myself — happily married, with twin sons. I decided to stay home full time with my babies, so I didn't take that perfect part-time job. But miraculously, last year, just as I was wishing for a ministry, the job came open again. My life is now balanced in a way I never dared hope it would be.

From time to time, I talk to women approaching 40 who are yearning for a baby. They're unsure, and they should be — it's a big decision to make. I tell them to listen to what their heart is telling them. It's important to gather a community of support to help with this process of discernment and with shaping the next steps.

And then, hoist your sails! The winds of God can amaze you! ⋘

40

Be in complete denial

There is no reason you can't ask for an extension on your decade deadline, argues journalist Mark Anderson. Stave it off until you feel comfortable with the big 4-0.

by Mark Anderson

Author and journalist Mark Anderson has an M.S in astrophysics and is quietly enjoying bending time in his thirty-teens till he checks off all the remaining items on his to-do-by-40 list. Already checked off are his first book, *"Shakespeare" By Another Name* (Gotham Books, 2005) and articles for a host of publications including *Wired, New Scientist, Plenty, Rolling Stone,* and *Harper's.*

We've all done it. In college, I did it a lot. In high school, a few times. My first girlfriend, I discovered, didn't really like doing it at all. We later broke up.

I'm talking, of course, about asking for extensions. On term papers, on deadlines, on sundry assignments within academia and without.

As I write these words, I'm enjoying the 303rd day after my 39th birthday. Two months hence, I plan to proudly celebrate my 30-10th birthday.

Some may choose to call it 40. Not me. Not yet.

Mind you, I'm actually looking forward to my 40s and 50s and however many other years and decades my body and continually advancing medical technology are able to yield up. But one or two goals (for instance, the screenplay that'll never be produced) remain to be completed. And 40 is as good a milestone as any to demand it by.

Yet, realistically, two months is not enough time to get to checking off those remaining check-boxes. So I'm applying for an extension.

Here's the wonderful thing, though. Unlike the hard-nosed professors who never believed that story about your term paper becoming the accidental cage-liner for your roommate's pet parakeet, you are guaranteed to receive this extension. All you need to do is ask.

A paradise of pleasures awaits you when you harness the wonderful and transformative power of denial.

To be clear, I'm not advocating denial-junkie binges like the kind you might see practiced by leather-skinned 60-something Southern Californians pretending they're hot mamacitas and papacitas not a day over 22. There is, obviously, such a thing as denial overdose.

I'm talking about the judicious and measured use of denial, in self-scrutinized proportions. Kids: You don't need to try this at home. Grownups: Knock yourselves out.

If you're on the verge of a milestone year, and you want to give yourself a year — or three — fudge factor, then do it! What the hell. If you don't care, who's going to?

You may very well spend that year or three being more productive now than when you're under a real, no-fooling-around-this-time deadline. And even if you don't use the time as productively as you might, at the end of your fudge time, you'll have lived in the skin of a chronologically (in my case) 40-something long enough to know that 40-something really isn't such a big deal after all.

Denial is one of those monkey wrenches in our mind's toolbox that we can use, or abuse, as we please. But just because we all can probably think of a dozen or more people who are guilty of denial abuse, doesn't mean there aren't also plenty of examples of more carefully measured denial use, too.

Denial, applied in moderation, helps us to stave off the inevitable long enough to become acquainted with it and get to know it on a first-name basis. In the case of those decade-years of our life, denial can be a great mellowing agent.

After the turbulence of the oh-god-I'm-not-a-teenager-anymore 20th birthday (followed ever so quickly by the oh-god-I'm-a-quarter-century), I found that life moves much more smoothly when I ease into a decade. Sort of like sliding into second base. After all, they're just arbitrary divisions of time anyway. Decades are nothing more than a byproduct of an effectively random fluke of evolution: Our species has five digits on each of two hands. As a result, we group our numbers in batches of 10 — not 8 or 12 or 23.

What am I talking about? If you grew up in the U.S. and are now somewhere in the neighborhood of 4-...er...30-10, you'll probably recall those fabulous Saturday morning cartoons from the 1970s called "Schoolhouse Rock." As Bob Dorough says in his song "Little Twelvetoes":

"Now if man had been born with six fingers on each hand, he'd also have 12 toes or so the theory goes..."

Dorough goes on to say that a person with 12 fingers would naturally count by dozens and so the attendant counting system would be based on that; ergo, if we set up our numbering system accordingly, what we five-fingered creatures call someone's 40th birthday would instead be reckoned as 34. Big whoop.

Now, you see that? There you have one perfect example of a blatant attempt to rationalize away a potentially uncomfortable fact. It's pure, unadulterated denial. Isn't it sweet?

[http://www.schoolhouserock.tv/Little.html]

About the Commissioning Editor

Allison Kyle Leopold, COMMISSIONING EDITOR, is an award-winning editor and journalist, owner/editor-in-chief of AKL Studio, a magazine and book development company, and Editorial Director for R/GA. She has authored more than a dozen books. Leopold began her career with *Seventeen* before joining *Harper's Bazaar* and *Vogue* magazines. She was Editor of *Country Living Gardener* and *Country Living Holidays*, Editor of special interest lifestyle publications for *Woman's Day*, and editor-in-chief of *Flair* magazine. She is an adjunct professor at Fashion Institute of Technology, State University of New York.

Credits:

Take me at face value © 2007 Tawni O'Dell; *Pause for reflection* © 2007 Nigel Marsh; *Embrace your inner passion* © 2007 Shari Caudron; *Midlife: don't call it a crisis* © 2007 Tim Hall; *Don't be a jerk* © 2007 Steve Belanger; *Ask your heart, not your head, where to go from here* © 2007 Scott Chesney; *Divine your own right* © 2007 Divinity to Infinity; *Renovate! (your inner spirit and your home)* © 2007 Michael Ruhlman; *Call your friends and say "I love you"* © 2007 Sophronia Scott; *Move mountains* © 2007 Alison Levine; *Seize the dreams of your youth* © 2007 Steve Doppelt; *Take the entrepreneurial plunge* © 2007 Sarah Butterworth; *Go back to work* © 2007 Tina Grant; *Stop doing things you don't enjoy* © 2007 Marcus Buckingham; *Be the mother of reinvention* © 2007 Julia Roberts; *Bounce back at 40* © 2007 Christopher Blake Mays; *Get strong* © 2007 Lisa Hoffman; *Defy your age* © 2007 Edward Vilga; *Use a midlife crisis to transform yourself* © 2007 Lisa Sattler; *Give lifelong care to the skin you're in* © 2007 Kenneth Beer, MD; *Stop stressing out* © 2007 Diana Winston; *Have a heart to heart with your parents* © 2007 Miriam Rabkin, MD; *Take a swing at golf* © 2007 Michelle McGann; *Obsess and reassess* © 2007 Jonathan Ames; *Enough already — get ready for retirement!* © 2007 Michael Falcon; *Protect the best years of your life* © 2007 Angelia Fritter; *Open doors. Change the world. Volunteer.* © 2007 Brian Walsh; *Make art a part of your life* © 2007 Brook S. Mason; *Throw a fabulous party* © 2007 David Tutera; *Do yourself (and the world) a favor: learn to live with less* © 2007 Harry Allen; *Don't dye your hair* © 2007 Elizabeth Peavey; *Color your future* © 2007 Leslie Harrington PhD; *Grow a garden* © 2007 Deborah Needleman; *What to know about turning 40* © 2013 Samantha Ettus; *Power up your activism* © 2007 Lisa Renstrom; *Have a bun and a pizza in the oven* © 2007 Amy Scherber; *Connect with your landscape* © 2007 Douglas M. Thompson; *Seek the spirit — and find it* © 2007 Pamela Barz; *Be in complete denial* © 2007 Mark Kendall Anderson.